PHP Programming For Affiliate Marketers

By: John Elder
JohnElder.org

PHP Programming For Affiliate Marketers

By: John Elder

Published By Avery & Co. Publishing
New York, NY USA

ISBN 0-9725604-5-9

First Edition

All material contained in this book is for informational purposes only and is no substitute for professional advice. Neither John Elder, Flatplanet Media, LLC or it's affiliates (collectively referred to as COMPANY) make any guarantees of the tactics or strategies described in this book. Successful use of any tactic or strategy described in this book depends on the specific person, their experience, and their business and marketing ability. COMPANY makes no claims or guarantees regarding income generated from the use of any tactic or strategy described in this book. Reader agrees to indemnify and hold COMPANY harmless from and against any and all claims, demands, liabilities, expenses, losses, damages, attorney fees arising from any and all claims and lawsuits for libel, slander, copyright, and trademark violation as well as all other claims resulting from reading this book.

A Note From The Author

If you find any typos or grammatical errors in this book, they're there for a reason. Some people like searching for them and I aim to please! If you find one and want to let me know, you can contact me at **www.flatplanetmedia.com/contact**

A SPECIAL REQUEST

If you enjoy this book, would you head back to Amazon.com and leave a quick review or click the "like" button at the top of the page?

(http://www.amazon.com/PHP-Programming-Affiliate-Marketers-ebook/dp/B00A2TTNR0)

Reviews are incredibly important to us independent authors. Just one or two can vault our books up the list at Amazon.com

I'd certainly appreciate it!

-John Elder
JohnElder.org

Table Of Contents

About The Author

John Elder is a freelance web developer and entrepreneur who lives in Chicago. He works mainly with PHP and Mysql, HTML and CSS, and a little Javascript now and then. He also develops desktop software using Visual Basic, and dabbles from time to time in Ruby and Python.

To view his portfolio of past projects, visit:
http://www.johnelder.org/portfolio

To hire John for free lance coding, visit:
http://www.flatplanetmedia.com/hire-me-as-a-coder

Introduction

Hello and welcome to PHP Programming for Affiliate Marketers! You've taken the first step into the glamorous and exciting world of PHP programming. I think it's safe to say that nothing in your life will ever be the same again.

Yeah.

Before we get into anything else, here's my contact information. If you have any questions about anything you read here, feel free to drop me an email anytime.

You can contact me at
http://www.JohnElder.org/contact

Just fill out the form and shoot me an message. I check my email constantly so if you need clarification on something you read, don't quite understand something, or just want to shoot the breeze, send me a message.

Who This Book Is Written For

This is a strange hybrid sort of book. On one hand it's about computer programming, but it's not really aimed at computer programmers, or anyone with any skills in programming whatsoever...

It's aimed at affiliate marketers.

Why affiliate marketers? Because I am one - and over the years I've greatly enhanced my businesses with the judicial use of PHP on my web sites.

I run an Affiliate Marketing blog at **MarketingFool.com** where I teach my Adsense and Affiliate Marketing methods (I've been earning 100% of my income online since around 1996).

More and more the methods I talk about involve bits and pieces of PHP code on my websites...

...things like randomly showing different types of Adsense ads, spinning text on different web pages, all the way to creating complex website frameworks that allow me to scale thousands of websites with the click of a button.

The more I tought my methods at MarketingFool.com, the more people started scratching their heads because they didn't understand the PHP programming involved.

I have a programming background. I've been coding since I was eight years old. But most people don't have a coding background.

Yet using PHP can greatly increase the effectiveness of their websites.

That's why I decided to write this book.

You don't need any prior programming experience. I'm going to walk you through everything you'll need to start using PHP on your websites.

By the time you're finished with this book, you'll have a pretty decent understanding of PHP programming basics.

Let's Define Affiliate Marketing

First off, what is Affiliate Marketing?

Wikipedia defines it as:

"...a type of performance-based marketing in which a business rewards one or more affiliates for each visitor or customer brought about by the affiliate's own marketing efforts. The industry has four core players: the merchant (also known as 'retailer' or 'brand'), the network (that contains offers for the affiliate to choose from and also takes care of the payments), the publisher (also known as 'the affiliate'), and the customer. The market has grown in complexity to warrant a secondary tier of players, including affiliate management agencies, super-affiliates and specialized third party vendors.

Affiliate marketing overlaps with other Internet marketing methods to some degree, because affiliates often use regular advertising methods. Those methods include organic search engine optimization (SEO), paid search engine marketing (PPC - Pay Per Click), e-mail marketing, and in some sense display advertising. On the other hand, affiliates sometimes use less orthodox techniques, such as publishing reviews of products or services offered by a partner."

Uh...I guess that's a definition. In my mind Affiliate Marketing is the act of promoting someone else's products or services and earning a commission whenever you sell something.

For instance, I might build a website about Baby Strollers with lots of great stuff about Baby Strollers (info, pictures, prices, etc). When someone clicks on a link to buy one of the strollers on my website, the link leads them to that product being sold on Amazon.com.

When they purchase it, Amazon pays me a commission...usually around 7%.

My affiliate websites usually have lots of Adsense ads on them too. If someone clicks on one of those ads, Google pays me anywhere from a few pennies up to a few dollars depending on what advertisers are willing to pay for each specific ad.

Because of that, I like to glump Adsense into Affiliate Marketing, though technically they're not really all that related.

So there you have it.

When building my Baby Stroller website, I need all kinds of tricks; and PHP gives me the tools I need.

What About Wordpress?

Wordpress is a great platform and a lot of Affiliate Marketers use it to build their websites because it's very easy to use and requires little to no programming experience.

The problem is, it's fairly hard to scale wordpress because it's a massive resource hog and takes up lots of webhosting disk space and bandwidth.

If you're building a handful of sites, it's fine. But if you're building a network of dozens or hundreds (or even thousands) of websites, it's impossible.

Many times, in order to make a lot of money with affiliate marketing you need to build a large network of websites. This is especially true when it comes to Adsense websites.

In the example above, I might make a handful of dollars a day with my Baby Stroller websites. If I want to make more money, I need to build more websites focused on different types of products.

In other words, I need to scale my operations.

In such cases, it's much easier to hand code your websites with regular HTML and CSS and some judicious use of PHP for certain things.

If you have no experience with building websites by hand with HTML and CSS (and without Wordpress) you have a couple options.

1. Hire a designer. It's easy to find cheap ones for basic projects at elance or fiver.

2. Learn HTML and CSS. It's not that hard really, there are tons of free resources out there for learning. I recommend you take the free "Web Fundamentals" course at Codecademy.com It's online, interactive, easy to follow, and a great way to learn HTML and CSS at your own pace.

Even if you decide to use Wordpress, you can still use many of the things I'll teach you in this book. I'll show you how later in the book.

With Me So Far?

So now we know what an affiliate marketer is, and we know that this book is aimed at people with absolutely no programming experience whatsoever.

There's nothing left to do but dive in and get started...

Actually, there's one more thing. Before we get started I want to point you towards a great PHP resource that you'll want to familiarize yourself with (especially after you read this book).

It's called PHP.net and more specifically:
http://www.php.net/manual/en/langref.php

There you'll find the PHP manual with countless code examples, instructions, and basically everything you need whenever you get stuck or can't remember some little thing about PHP.

Whenever I need get stumped writing code, I'll run a Google search for whatever I'm stumped on. PHP.net is usually the first listing that pops up.

For instance, if I couldn't remember the exact syntax for an IF/ELSE statement, I'd go to Google and type in "IF/ELSE PHP" and the first listing to pop up is the PHP.net manual page that talks about IF/ELSE statements.

So learn to love PHP.net! It's an invaluable resource.

And now...let's get started!

CHAPTER ONE

HTML And FTP Basics

Before we get into PHP, we need to spend just a few minutes familiarizing ourselves with HTML, otherwise you'll be completely lost...

Don't worry, I'm not going to teach you HTML, you just need to be able to recognize it and understand a few basic concepts.

So What Is HTML?

HTML (or Hyper Text Markup Language) is the building block of the Internet. It's the programming language (if you could call it that) that's used to build web pages.

Whenever you browse a website, you can view that site's html by "Viewing The Page Source". Usually web browsers have a button on the menu you can click for that.

If you're using the Chrome or Firefox web browser, just put the mouse anywhere on the web page and right click the mouse button and choose "View Page Source".

The thing that pops up is HTML. You should try to learn HTML if possible. It's really easy and the more you know, the easier things will be when building your web sites.

Why do you need to learn this stuff? Because we'll be using PHP in conjunction with HTML. The HTML document is where you type in the PHP code I'll be teaching you.

So you need to at least be familiar with a basic HTML document.

Let's take a look at one:

```
<!DOCTYPE html>
<html>
 <head>
  <title>Hello World!</title>
 </head>
 <body>

  <center>
  <H1>Hello World, This Is A Web Page!</H1>
  <br/>
  This is a simple example
  <br/>
  of a basic web page. Whee!!
 </center>

 </body>
</html>
```

This is a VERY primitive website, but should give you an idea of what they look like. The example code above would produce a web page that looks like this:

Pretty basic, but you get the idea.

To make that webpage appear on the Internet you would type that code into a text file using a program like notepad on your computer, then save the file with an .html extension.

So if you had a website called www.yoursite.com and wanted to name that page "page", you would save the file in notepad as page.html and then upload it to your web host using FTP (file transfer protocol) software.

Once uploaded, you could direct your web browser to www.yoursite.com/page.html and the picture above is what you'd see.

Getting Back To The HTML Code...

Take a look at the code...there's not really much to it. HTML is mostly made up of tags... things between < and >. I won't get into all of them, because that's not the point of this book; but some common ones that you'll come across are:

<h1>Big Headers</h1>

<h2>Slightly Smaller Headers</h2>

<h3>Even Smaller Hearders</h3>

<strong>Bold Text</strong>

<em>Italics text</em>

<center>Center text on the middle of the page</center>

<a href="page.html">A Hyperlink</a>

<img src="image.jpg"> (adds an image to the page)

*
New Line*

<p>New Paragraph

You'll notice that most have opening *and* closing tags (like <h1></h1>). In those cases, the text inside of the tags is the thing that's being effected.

Some tags don't have closing tags...things like <br> which adds a new line, or the <img src=""> tag that adds an image to the page.

The more you learn about and work with HTML, the more you'll get used to the different tags. I do recommend you grab yourself a HTML book, or read an online tutorial or two just to familiarize yourself with it. I highly recommend the free "Web Fundamentals" course at Codecademy.com Their website is set up like a game that you play. Its fun and easy.

HTML and PHP Go Together...

I don't want to start talking about PHP just yet (we'll start in the next chapter), but PHP uses a similar tag structure, which is one of the reasons why I'm familiarizing you with HTML now.

For example, this bit of PHP code will add the date to a web page, well specifically the year (like 2013):

```
<?php echo date('Y'); ?>
```

See how similar it is to the HTML tags? But I'm getting ahead of myself, we'll get into PHP in the next chapter. Right now I just want to point out the similarities and show how PHP fits in to html.

Let's take our original HTML example. Imagine we'd like to programatically enter the date on our example webpage above. You would simply copy that line of PHP code into our HTML example code like this:

```
<!DOCTYPE html>
<html>
 <head>
  <title>Hello World!</title>
 </head>
 <body>

  <center>
  <H1>Hello World, This Is A Web Page!</H1>
  <br/>
  This is a simple example
  <br/>
  of a basic web page. Whee!!
  <br/><br/>
  Copyright &copy; <?php echo date('Y'); ?>
 </center>

 </body>
</html>
```

(Notice the php code in bold above). And we'd get this:

Notice also that we had to change the name of the file from page.html to page.php in order to start using PHP code on it. That's a normal convention.

So PHP goes hand in glove with HTML, which is why you should become as familiar with HTML as possible.

But you certainly don't need to become a master HTML wizard. Just learn enough to be able to identify things for now.

Most affiliate marketers are familiar with Wordpress and not really familiar with uploading HTML files to a web host. You should also learn to use FTP software so that you can upload your files to your webhost.

FileZilla FTP Software

I like to use the free FileZilla ftp program. You can download a copy at **http://filezilla-project.org/**

When you go to their website, there are two download options; client and server. You want to download the "client" version.

FTP software can seem intimidating at first, especially if the only thing you've ever worked with before is Wordpress.

But really it's very very simple and I'm going to walk you through it right now.

After you download and install FileZilla, run it. At the very top left hand corner of the screen you'll see a little icon:

Click that little icon and this screen will pop up:

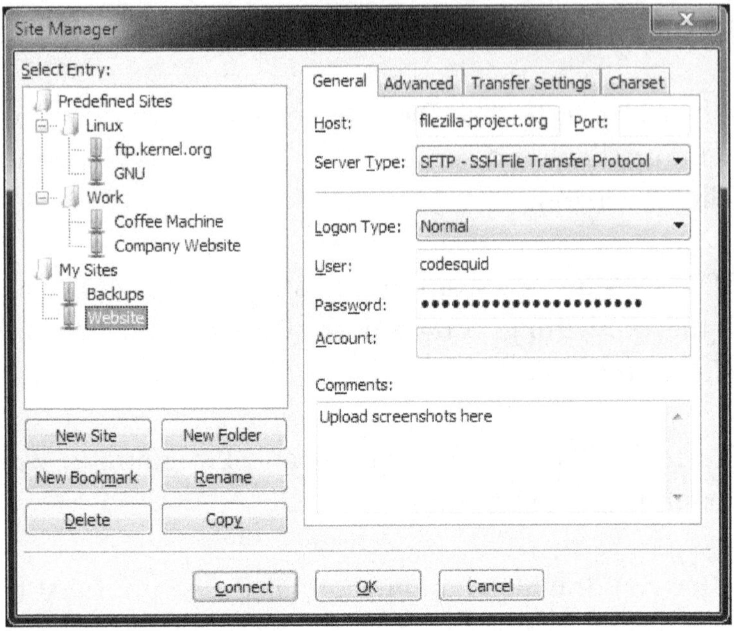

That's called the "Site Manager" and it's where you type in your webhosting account details.

In the "Host" field, type in the URL of your website. My website is http://www.JohnElder.org so I would type that into that field.

Under that, select "Normal" in the "Logon Type:" field.

Under that type in your webhosting username in the "Username" field, and type your password in the "Password" field.

Your webhosting provider will have given you those two things when you set up your account. Usually they email it to you in a welcome email when you create the account.

After you've typed in your webhosting information, just click the "Connect" button at the bottom of the screen.

The software should then do it's thing and whiz bang connect to your web hosting account.

Next you should see this screen:

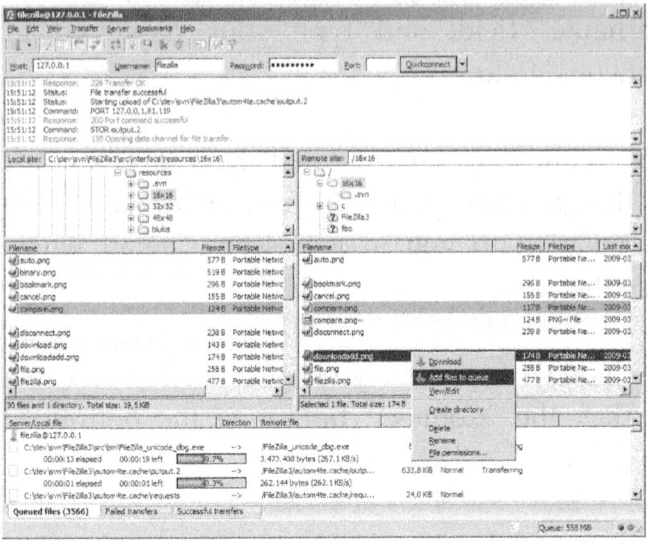

It can seem a little intimidating, but it's really not. What we're looking at is a simple two-panel screen.

On the left hand side of the screen is your own computer file system. You can click around the top panel on the left side to navigate to any directory on your computer.

On the right hand side is your webhosting account.

Remember when we created that page.php HTML file earlier? To transfer that file to your webhosting account, you would just click around on the left hand side till you navigated to the directory in which you saved the file on your computer.

Then you'd see that file listed in the middle panel of the left side of the screen.

After that, you'd just double click that page.php file and it would be transferred to your webhost. It should then pop up on right hand side of the screen. That's all there is to it! Here's a breakdown...

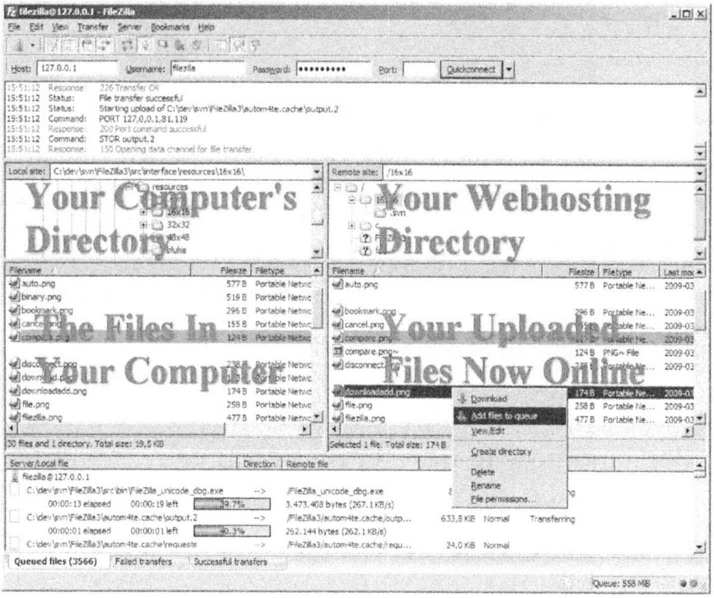

Pretty simple! Just remember, the left hand side is your computer, and the right hand side is your webhost.

One thing to note, you should check with your webhost to find out WHERE they want you to upload files. You'll notice at the top of the right hand column a field that says "Remote Site:" followed by a box with a file path written in it.

Each webhost is different. One webhost may want you to upload your files to the /home directory on the server.

Another might want you to upload your files to the /home/www directory or the /users/public_html directory.

Usually a webhost will have a support page on their website that tells you that, or they'll spell it out in the welcome email that they send you when you first open your account.

Summing It All Up...

So now you're passingly familiar with HTML, and you understand how to transfer files from your computer to your web host via FTP...the only thing to do is dive into PHP. So let's get right to it!

CHAPTER TWO

PHP Basics

What Is PHP?

Before we learn how to use PHP, we should take a minute to talk about what it is....you know, just for fun.

PHP is a server side scripting language that's most often used to create dynamic web pages (pages that can change on the fly based on different things like user interaction and things like that).

Many other programming languages need to be called from an external file in order to work, but PHP code is embedded directly into an HTML document like we learned earlier.

That makes it incredibly useful in creating dynamic web sites... it also makes it pretty easy to use.

What do I mean by a dynamic website? Well, let's say you wanted the days date to be shown on your website. You wouldn't want to log into your website everyday and update the date by hand, would you?

With a simple bit of PHP code, the site will update itself *dynamically* ("automatically" might be a better word for it) every day and show the current date.

There are many great books and online tutorials about PHP and if you're really into this I suggest you pick one up and really learn it.

For this book though, I'm not really going to teach you much in depth PHP, I'm just going to teach you enough so that you feel comfortable using it on your own website, and show you a few useful bits of code that you can copy and paste when you need them.

Why have I decided to take this approach? For one reason, there's a lot of really good PHP books out there already that can frankly teach you the ins and outs of the language better than I could.

But more specifically, I've decided to take this approach because this book is aimed at Affiliate Marketers, not programmers. Chances are, you have little to no programming background, and this way is just much easier for you.

I'm going to teach you some programming basics, I'll explain basic concepts like Variables and Arrays, but mostly we'll just stick to simple examples that you can copy and paste directly onto your website.

PHP Basics

So let's just dive in and start learning the basics of PHP.

As I mentioned in the last chapter, PHP code is written directly into an HTML document. When you want to use PHP on a web page, you need to change the extension of the file to .php

So if your page was called index.html before and you want to start using PHP on it, you need to rename it index.php.

Web servers can be modified so that you don't HAVE to rename the file with a .php extension, but that's a little beyond the scope of this book (at least at this point). For now, just assume you need to slap a .php onto the end of your HTML file names.

So let's break down the basic syntax of PHP code.

```
<?php echo 'Hello World'; ?>
```

Can you guess what that line of code does? Yep, you guessed it...it print's Hello World onto the screen.

The "Hello World" code is the universal first program that every programmer learns in any programming language. In PHP it's just that easy.

But let's break it down.

PHP's Delimiters

All PHP code is written and executed between what we call delimiters. The delimiters are:

```
<?php
```

and

```
?>
```

Any PHP code you ever want to use will be wrapped in those two delimiters, and won't work unless you use them.

In our example code, I've written it all on one line:

```
<?php echo 'Hello World'; ?>
```

But you don't have to. As long as you slap the delimiters on there, you can write the code on as many lines as you like. So we could just as easily have written the code like this:

```
<?php

echo 'Hello World';

?>
```

It's all the same to PHP.

Next the 'echo' command just tells PHP to echo (print to the screen) whatever is about to follow; in this case it's Hello World.

Quotation Marks In PHP

Next we see the 'Hello World'; bit. Notice that I used single quotation marks. I could also have used regular double quotation marks (") like this:

```
<?php echo "Hello World"; ?>
```

Believe it or not, the distinction is very important. PHP handles single and double quotation marks differently.

You use double quotes (") when you need to execute a variable inside the code and single quotes (') when you just want PHP to print whatever's in the quotation marks.

That's not going to make a whole lot of sense right now, but it will soon. For now, just remember that quotation marks are treated differently based on whether they're double or single.

The Semi-colon

Finally, notice the semi-colon after 'Hello World'

```
<?php echo 'Hello World'; ?>
```

PHP requires a semi-colon at the end of every statement. If your code doesn't work, chances are you forgot to slap a semi-colon at the end of some statement somewhere.

Last we have the closing ?> delimiter.

That's the basic structure and syntax of PHP. It's pretty straight forward. Believe me, some programming languages can get pretty goofy with their syntax, but PHP is pretty laid back and easy to use.

Comments in PHP

All programming languages treat comments a little differently. Comments are useful so that your code is readable by humans.

You'll know what your code is supposed to do when you write it today; but when you look at it again a year from now (when you need to modify it for one reason or another) and chances are, you'll have forgotten what it's supposed to do.

That's why commenting your code is so important. Don't go overboard, but its a good idea to add little comments that explain what each major part of your code does.

PHP has three ways to add comments:

/* */ for blocks and inline comments

// for one line comments

```
# also for one line comments
```

So let's give an example of each of those methods using our Hello World line of code:

```
<?php echo 'Hello World'; // prints Hello World to the screen ?>
```

```
<?php echo 'Hello World'; # prints Hello World to the screen ?>
```

```
<?php echo 'Hello World';
/* Prints
Hello World
to
the
screen */
?>
```

Each of those bits of code do the same thing. It doesn't matter which one you choose, it's really just a matter of personal style. Some coders like to use // and some like #. Still others like to user the /* and */ and type lots of comments between them.

Just remember that anything you write after the comment code (either // or # or /*) won't be interpreted by PHP.

In real life, we wouldn't have written a comment for our Hello World code because it's so very simple. As your code gets more complicated and longer, try to get in the habit of writing little one line comments to explain what your code is attempting to do.

For instance you might comment something like:

// chooses a random sized Adsense ad to print to the screen.

// spins this block of text

// adds a twitter feed to the web page

// Switches between Amazon and Shopzilla Affiliate Listings

You get the idea. Just comment on major things so that if you need to jolt your memory in the future, you'll be able to.

Comments aren't just for you. You might hire someone in the future to handle your code and they'll need to understand what your code is supposed to do.

With programming, there's never just one way to do a thing. Everyone writes code a little differently to do different things. That's why commenting your code is so important.

That pretty much wraps up the basics. In the next chapter I'm going to expand and teach you some basic fundamental programming concepts that you'll need to learn in order to do anything fun with PHP.

We'll get into Variables, Arrays, IF/Then Statements, Comparison Operators, and maybe Functions.

It's totally programming stuff, but you really should be exposed to it if you want to really get into PHP and programming in general.

I promise it won't be too bad!

So let's dive right in...

CHAPTER THREE

PHP Programming Concepts

Now it's time to really get into the meat of programming with PHP. When it comes to programming languages, they all have a backbone of similar concepts that are pretty much universal.

While the concepts are universal, each programming language treats them a little differently. The biggest part of learning a new programming language is learning how that specific language handles the concepts I'm about to teach you.

So in some ways this may be the most important chapter of the book. Some of you may love it, others may just skim over it. It really depends on how serious you are about learning how to program.

If you're reading this book to get some useful code snippets to add to your affiliate web pages, then this chapter is going to be massive overkill.

If, on the other hand, you're really into this and want to learn how to program properly; then this chapter is for you.

I'm going to be discussing several concepts in this chapter, namely;

- Variables
- Comparison Operators
- If / Then Statements
- Loops: For and While

- Randomizing
- Arrays
- Functions

If you understand these concepts, you'll be well on your way to becoming a proper programmer.

Variables

The first programming concept most people learn are variables. Think of variables as empty buckets.

You can put things into them. Words, numbers, strings of many words, lists...all kinds of good things.

In PHP variables are created by slapping a dollar sign in front of a word, like this $variable.

Once you stick something into a variable, you can pull it out and display it whenever you want just by calling the variable. It's incredibly handy.

Let's write an example. Let's say we've got a website about Golf Clubs. Let's put the term "Golf Clubs" into a variable called main_keyword:

```
<?php $main_keyword = 'Golf Clubs'; ?>
```

That's all there is to it. Now any time you want to display that keyword on your webpage, you'd just print this line of code:

```
<?php echo $main_keyword; ?>
```

Pretty simple!

Why would we want to do that? Isn't that more work than just writing the keyword "Golf Clubs" on your webpage?

There's tons of reasons to do it with PHP instead. What happens if you want to change the main keyword later. Maybe you discover that the search engines prefer the phrase "Cheap Golf Clubs" for SEO reasons.

Instead of going through your entire website and manually changing each instance of the phrase "Golf Clubs" to the new phrase "Cheap Golf Clubs", you can just change your original php declaration from:

```
<?php $main_keyword = "Golf Clubs"; ?>
```

to

```
<?php $main_keyword = "Cheap Golf Clubs"; ?>
```

Now everywhere on your web page that has a <?php echo $main_keyword; ?> tag will now show "Cheap golf Clubs".

It's easy to create a file that holds all the variables you want to use throughout your website. That way when you want to update all the pages of your website, all you have to do is update that one variable file.

I'll show you exactly how to do that in a later chapter.

Fun With Variables

Like I said, you can put all kinds of things into a variable. Numbers are a common sort of thing to stick in there.

```
<?php $my_variable = "41"; ?>
```

If you put numbers into variables, you can do all sorts of math type things to them. Things like add, subtract, multiply, divide, etc. Its pretty simple.

```
<?php echo $my_variable * 2; ?>
```

Would print "82" to the screen (41 times 2). Math operators are exactly what you would expect them to be, namely:

+ (for adding)

- (for subtracting)
* (for multiplying)
/ (for dividing)

I'll talk more about these later when I discuss comparison operators (things like equal to, not equal to, greater than, less than, etc).

Variables can also be assigned to other variables! For instance:

```
<?php
$main_keyword = "Golf Clubs";
$second_keyword = $main_keyword;
?>
```

In that example, both $main_keyword and $second_keyword are set to the phrase "Golf Clubs".

You can also string together keywords by using the period like this:

```
<?php
$main_keyword = "Golf Clubs";
$second_keyword = "Cheap";

echo "$second_keyword " . "$main_keyword";
```

```
?>
```

In that example "Cheap Golf Clubs" would be printed to the screen. Notice how I used double quotations marks?

I did that so that a space would be printed between our two variables. See how I typed a space after $second_keyword and its quotation mark?

If I simply typed:

```
echo $second_keyword . $main_keyword;
```

Then the webpage would print CheapGolf Clubs without a space. So just keep that in mind.

Notice how I break up variable names with the underscore _ like in main_keyword. There's no real reason to do that. It's just a matter of style.

It makes it easier to read your code if you do that but there's no rule that says you have to do that when naming variables. But it's a best practice and I recommend you do the same.

Really that's all there is to variables. BY FAR variables will be the thing you use PHP for the most.

When I build a website, I like to template everything out. I'll get into templating later on. Variables allow me to create dozens, or even hundreds of websites based on one template.

To make each website different, I just change the variables in the variable file (I'll show you how to do that later). Just by swapping out the variables in the variable file, a Golf Club website can become a Baby Stoller website.

...And that's one of the reasons why learning PHP is so important to an Affiliate Marketer who needs to build many different websites.

But I'm getting ahead of myself. We'll get into those more advanced topics later on. For now let's stick to the basic programming concepts.

PHP Comparison Operators

The next programming concept I want to share with you is the comparison operator.

I briefly touched on them when talking about variables earlier. Comparison Operators allows you to...make comparisons between two or more variables.

They mostly deal with numbers, but they can also deal with text as well.

In PHP, the main comparison operators are (assuming we have two variables names $a and $b):

$a == $b (\$a is equal to $b)

$a === $b (\$a is identical to $b)

$a != $b (\$a is NOT equal to $b)

$a !== $b (\$ is NOT identical to $b)

$a <> $b (another way to do $a is NOT equal to $b)

$a < $b (\$a is less than $b)

$a > $ b (\$a is greater than $b)

$a <= $b ($a is less than or equal to $b)

$a >= $b ($a is greater than or equal to $b)

There are probably others as well, but those are the main ones that you're going to come across.

Most of those are fairly straight forward math operations that you're probably already familiar with.

The one that probably needs some explaining is the == equal comparator. It trips up people all the time because your instinct is to use a single = equal sign instead of the double == one.

The reason why you can't us a single equal sign is because we use the single equal sign to declare a variable.

Remember earlier when we declared our variables?

<?php $main_keyword = "Golf Clubs"; ?>

The single equal sign is used to show what's in a variable. The double equal sign == is used to make comparisons.

For example, you might want to ask; "Is our $main_keyword variable Golf Clubs?" and to do that you would use the double equal sign:

```
<?php
if ($main_keyword == "Golf Clubs")
  { echo "Yes our main keyword is Golf Clubs"; }
?>
```

Don't be thrown by the new "if" code...we'll get into that later. For now just realize that this code is asking "Is our main_keyword Golf Clubs"?

I'll talk about IF/THEN statements next, they're pretty important (but still pretty easy as you can see above).

But let's get back to comparison operators.

There's tons of reasons why you're going to use comparison operators as an affiliate marketer.

For instance, you might assign a cookie to a user that creates a simple counter. Every time that person visits a new page on your site, the counter might increase by one.

Maybe after a person has visited 10 pages of your site, you want to pop up a special offer, or a newsletter subscription form, or a new set of advertisements.

Comparator Operators to the rescue.

Or you might use them when auto generating keywords on a page. If the number of keywords listed is less than 20, add another keyword from the list.

Etc etc etc. There are too many possibilities to discuss and we'll get into specific examples later.

In the mean time, just make sure you understand the basic concept of comparator operators. They're a way to compare two or more variables. Piece of cake!

IF/THEN Statements

The logical next concept to learn after comparison operators is the IF/THEN statement. It's a common element of any programming language and something you'll use ALL the time.

If the comparator operators allow you to make comparisons between two variables, the IF/THEN statement DOES something based on the outcome of those comparisons.

If 2 is greater than 1, do this...

If our main_keyword is "Golf Clubs", do that...

It's incredibly useful.

Let's take a look at the IF/THEN code we just saw:

```
<?php
if ($main_keyword == "Golf Clubs")
  { echo "Yes our main keyword is Golf Clubs"; }
?>
```

In this case; If $main_keyword is "Golf Clubs", then print out "Yes our main keyword is Golf Clubs" to the screen.

It's not too terribly complicated. IF/THEN statements are built like this:

```
<?php

if (TEST SOMETHING) {
        IF THE TEST IS TRUE, DO SOMETHING HERE;
}

?>
```

The thing between the parenthesis ( ) is the thing you're testing. That's where you're going to use your comparison operators.

Then IF the thing you tested between the parenthesis is TRUE, the stuff between the { and } get's executed.

If....this is true...then...do that

Let's take a look at a couple simple examples:

```
<?php if (100 > 2) {
 echo "Yes 100 is indeed  bigger than 2"; } ?>
```

By now you can probably guess what that bit of code does. It asks the question "Is 100 greater than 2?" and if so, prints out "Yes 100 is indeed bigger than 2".

Granted that's a really simple example let's make it a little more complicated and throw some variables in there.

In this next bit of code, let's pretend that there's a variable called $user_hit_count that increases by 1 every time a specific user views a new page of your site (let's pretend it creates a unique cookie on the users machine so that we can keep track of that person individually).

```
<?php  if ($user_hit_count > 10) {
  echo "<strong><center>Get 10% Off Your Purchase For
The Next 15 Minutes!! </strong></center>"; } ?>
```

In that bit of code, PHP will check to see if a person has visited your website more than 10 times, and if so will print out "Get 10% Off Your Purchase For The Next 15 Minutes!! in bold and centered text on the screen.

Of course, we'd need a lot more code to actually implement that (we'd need to write a bit of code to place a cookie, and increment the hit counter), but I'm just using it as an example to show you IF/THEN statements in action.

You can expand the IF/THEN statement to make it even more powerful by using an ELSE statement too.

IF/ELSE Statements

These are just like IF/THEN Statements but with a little added complexity.

Basically they ask IF something is true, DO Something, if its not true, do something else...

If true...do this. Else...do that.

The basic syntax is the same, you just lop an ELSE statement to the end like this:

```
<?php if (TEST SOMETHING) {
 DO SOMETHING; }
 else { IF Not True, Do This Instead; }
?>
```

It's pretty straight forward. Using our hit counter example above, adding an else statement would look like this:

```
<?php if ($user_hit_count > 10) {
 echo "<strong><center>Get 10% Off Your Purchase For
The Next 15 Minutes!! </strong></center>"; }
```

```
else { echo "The more you use our website, the more savings you receive!"; }

?>
```

In that code, when the hit counter is less than 10 "The more you use our website, the more savings you receive!" gets shown. As soon as the hit count hits 11 (greater than 10), then the bold centered text "Get 10% off your purchase..." is shown.

If true do this, else do that.

IF/ELSEIF Statements

So we've gone over IF/THEN and IF/ELSE statements, so prepare to have your mind blown...there's one more we need to touch on, the IF/ELSEIF Statement.

It's very much like the first two we discussed, just a little different. It's used to test several things, not just one. Sometimes you need to test more than one thing, IF/ELSEIF works great.

It looks like this:

```
<?php

if (TEST SOMETHING) {
 DO SOMETHING; }

elseif (TEST SOMETHING ELSE) {
 DO SOMETHING ELSE; }

else { DO SOMETHING ELSE: }

?>
```

Ok, that's a little more complicated, but not too bad really. The fun part is, you can slap in as many elseif's as you want. Need to test against 10 different things? Slap in 10 elseif's.

Confused? Let's look at a classic example:

```
<?php

if ($a > $b) {
   echo "a is bigger than b"; }

elseif ($a == $b) {
   echo "a is equal to b"; }

else {
   echo "a is smaller than b";
}
?>
```

Work your way through the code. What do you think is going to happen?

If $a is bigger than $b then "a is bigger than b" will be printed to the screen.

If $a is NOT bigger than $b, we drop down to the elseif statement, which asks; "is a equal to b?". If it is, then "a is equal to b" will be printed.

If $a is not bigger than $b and $a is not equal to $b, the final else will be executed and "a is smaller than b" will be printed to the screen.

So as you can see, a little more complicated but not too bad. It's a handy little tool to have at your disposal, but chances are you won't run into it all that much unless you really get into PHP programming.

Loops

Another basic concept in any programming language is a Loop. Loops let you check things over and over until some sort of condition is met, at which point the program does something else.

A big part of Loops is incrementing numbers. Often times when we loop through something, we'll add 1 to a counter to keep track of how many times we've looped through.

PHP has *Operators* that make incrementing easy. They're very similar to the Comparison Operators we learned earlier. In this case they're:

++ (increment by one)
-- (subtract by one)

So let's look at an example:

```
<?php
$a = 1;
$a++;
echo $a;
?>
```

In that example we have a variable $a that is set to the number 1. $a++ increments $a by one (adds 1). Then the last line prints the output to the screen...in this case it will print 2.

We could easily have written it as $a-- in which case the program would have subtracted 1 from $a and printed out 0.

With me so far? Good because we'll use that a lot in loops.

Back To Loops...

There are several different Loops in PHP but I'm just going to talk about a couple of the most common ones. First, let's look at the While Loop.

While Loop

Many people consider While Loops to be the simplest loops in PHP so they're a good place to start.

The concept of a while loop is pretty straight forward. It tells PHP to execute some code WHILE something else is true. Another way to think of it is, execute some code as long as something is true.

When the thing stops being true, stop executing the code. So you see, we're looping over a thing over and over, for as long as it remains true.

While Loops take this basic form:

```
<?php

while (expression) {
 statement;
}

?>
```

As you can see, they look very familiar...they look just like an IF/THEN or IF/ELSE statement, don't they! So you should be familiar with them already.

Let's look at an actual example:

```
<?php

$a = 1;
while ($a < 10) {
  echo $a++;
}

?>
```

So what are we looking at here? Can you guess what this code will do?

It starts out by declaring a variable $a to equal the number 1. Next our while loop tests to see if $a is less than 10 (which it is because 1 is definitely less than 10).

If $a is less than ten, it executes the next bit of code, printing $a to the screen and then incrementing it by 1 (remember $a++ increments by one).

Then it starts the loop all over again and checks to see if $a is less than 10. And keeps looping and incrementing until a is no longer less than 10.

So the first time the loop runs, it will print 1 to the screen and increment $a by one. The next time $a will be 2 because the code just incremented it by one. 2 is less than 10 so it will print 2 to the screen and increment it by 1...

$a becomes 3....3 is less than 10 so it prints 3 to the screen and then increments it by one...

$a becomes 4...4 is less than 10 so...you get the idea.

What is the last number that will be printed to the screen? Go on guess....

If you guessed 9, you're correct. Once $a becomes 9, the program will determine that 9 is less than 10, print 9 to the screen, then increment it by 1. $a then becomes 10.

The next time the loop runs, it will see that $a is 10, and 10 is NOT less than 10, so the program will end right then without printing 10 to the screen.

Infinite Loops

One thing you really need to be careful of is the infinite loop, which is a loop that just keeps looping and looping and looping forever because the initial expression never becomes true.

Let's look at our last bit of code and tweak it just a little to make it into an infinite loop. Can you discover what I did differently this time without comparing it to the last code to make it an infinite loop?

```
<?php

$a = 1;
while ($a < 10) {
 echo $a;
}

?>
```

Need a hint? Look at the echo $a; statement. Earlier, that line read: echo $a++; but this time I kept off the ++ part. Now the $a variable is never incremented...and stays the same...$a = 1!

So the program will check to see if $a is less than 10, which it is because $a is 1. It will then print 1 to the screen and loop through again. When it loops, it will find that $a still equals 1 and 1 is still less than 10, so it will print out 1 again.

In fact, it will continue to print out 1 1 1 1 1 1 1 1 1 1 1 1 1 1 1...well, forever. We're stuck in an infinite loop!

So be careful with loops! Keep an eye out for potential infinite loop madness.

For Loops

For Loops are a little trickier than While loops. People tend to have a little trouble wrapping their heads around them. They may be a little more complicated, but they aren't really that bad.

You're going to want to use a for loop whenever you know how many times you want the thing to loop.

For Loops look like this:

```
<?php

for (expression1; condition; increment) {
  statement }

?>
```

Expression1 is usually the beginning of your counter. The condition is usually the thing you're testing against, and the increment is the incrementation of the original counter.

Let's look at a basic example:

```
<?php

for ($a = 1; $a < 10; $a++) {
   echo $a;
}

?>
```

Can you figure out what's going on here? Its similar to our While example, but written a little differently.

It starts out by setting our counter (in this case the variable $a) to the number 1 ($a =1;).

Next it tests the condition, asking is $a less than 10?

If $a is not less than 10, the increment is initialized ($a++) which adds 1 to $a, and then prints out $a to the screen (echo $a;).

Then the loop runs the condition test again. This time $a = 2, which is less than 10, so $a gets incremented again, and again and again until $a is no longer less than 10.

That's really all there is to it.

Over time you'll get a feel for when to use a while loop or a for loop. Many times it really doesn't matter which you use, other times one will be more useful than the other.

Loops are a little trickier than some of the other things we've talked about so far. I'd say that they're some of the most complicated of the basic concepts that you'll have to learn.

It's ok if you're a little fuzzy on them at this point. Just make yourself as familiar with them as possible and remember that they're out there. You may need them someday!

Randomizing

All right, let's take a step back from the complicated stuff and spend a few minutes on something very very simple, yet incredibly useful.

Randomization.

I love randomizing things. I use it on a daily basis more than just about anything else. As an Affiliate Marketer, it's a fantastic tool that has a zillion uses.

And for SEO (Search Engine Optimization) purposes, it has no equal.

PHP let's you grab a random number very easily. Basically the structure to create a random number looks like this:

```
<?php
rand ( int $min , int $max );
?>
```

First we initialize the random function by typing in rand, then we pipe in the min number and the max number between the parenthesis.

That's useful because you rarely want just any random number, like 4,592,923...instead you're going to want a specific random number; say, between 1 and 20.

So let's give an example bit of code to pick a number between 1 and 20:

```
<?php
echo rand (1, 20);
?>
```

That will print out a number between 1 and 20 to the screen. So the number might be 1...it might be 20, or it might be any number in between 1 and 20.

We hardly ever want to print out a random number to the screen though, we usually need to generate a random number for internal use within our code. Here's how we can generate a random number and then assign it to a variable so that we can use it later:

```
<?php
$random_number = rand (1,20);
?>
```

Now we've assigned a random number between 1 and 20 and stored it in the $random_number variable. We can then do anything we want with that variable.

Say for instance that we have a list of 20 keywords and we want to list one of them at random on our webpage, to do that we'd need to pick a random number. Actually, I'll show you how to do that next when I talk about Arrays.

It may not seem like it now, but random numbers are very useful to be able to work with. Trust me on that. It'll become more clear and obvious as we go on and start using all this stuff in real concrete examples.

For now, tuck rand( ) away and remember it for later.

Arrays

Arrays are pretty useful too, but I've waited till now to discuss them because they're a little complicated. Some people have a hard time wrapping their brains around them.

Don't worry, we'll work it through and you should have no problem.

Remember Variables? I said that a Variable is like a bucket that you can put things in.

Well an Array is very similar. It's like a bucket with lots of compartments that allow you to put lots of different things in at the same time and then call them each out individually whenever you want.

They even look a lot like Variables, in fact an Array is really just a special type of Variable.

There are a few different types of Arrays, namely Numeric, Associative, and Multi-dimensional.

I'm just going to talk about Numeric and Associative Arrays. Multi-Dimensional Arrays are a little more complicated and you probably won't run into them doing basic PHP work.

Arrays are basically made up of two parts; a key and a value. This is especially true of Associative Arrays, while Numeric Arrays are a little different (the keys are *numeric* in numeric arrays).

Why two parts? Picture a big bucket. If you throw a bunch of stuff in there, you need to be able to identify each thing, so you give it a key.

Think of it as tagging each item you shove in there.

Numeric Arrays

Numeric Arrays are the most common and the ones that you'll be using most often. Like I said, their keys are numeric. That way, later on, you can say "Show me the 4th thing in the bucket"...

...which makes it fun to use our Random function that we just learned. I can make an Array of 20 keywords, then randomly select 1 to display on my webpage.... but I'm getting ahead of myself.

Let's look at a basic numeric Array setup:

```
<?php
$variable = array ("value 1", "value 2", "value 3", "value
4");
?>
```

Pretty straight forward, $variable is whatever you name the array, then the items between the quotation marks are the things you want to stick into the array.

Let's say we wanted to access the 2nd item in the array, we'd use this bit of code:

```
<?php
echo $variable[1];
?>
```

You just slap the number of the item you want to access between the [and the] next to $variable. But wait, I said we wanted to access the second item in our array. Why did I write $variable[1] then?

Because Array numbering stars with zero. So the first thing in the list is numbered 0, the second thing is 1, the third thing is 2 and so on. I know, it's a little goofy. Just roll with it.

So let's use an actual example. Here I'm going to create an array with 10 keywords for my Baby Stroller Website, then print out the 6th keyword to the screen:

```
<?php

$keywords = array ("Baby Strollers", "Cheap Baby Strollers", "Baby Stroller Sale", "Girls Baby Strollers", "Boys Baby Strollers", "Infant Baby Strollers", "Jogging Strollers", "Two-Seat Strollers", "Jumper Seat Strollers", "Graco Baby Strollers");

echo $keywords[5];
?>
```

Pretty simple. Just be sure to put each item between quotation marks and separate them with commas. Can you tell which keyword will get printed to the screen?

If you guessed: "Infinte Baby Strollers" you're correct! (remember to start counting at zero)

In fact, here's the key value for each of those items in the array (just so we're all on the same page):

Baby Strollers = 0
Cheap Baby Strollers = 1
Baby Stroller Sale =2
Girls Baby Strollers = 3
Boys Baby Strollers = 4
Infant Baby Strollers = 5
Jogging Strollers = 6
Two-Seat Strollers = 7
Jumper Seat Strollers = 8
Graco Baby Strollers = 9

So if we instead typed echo $keyword[8] we would get "Jumper Seat Stroller" etc.

Let's add in our random function that we learned earlier. Why would we want to print a random keyword on our web site? SEO reasons! Google loves pages that are always "updating" and "active".

Throw in a few randomization methods like this and Google thinks your site is constantly being updated when in reality, it's all automated.

Here's the same example code, but with a randomization tweak:

```
<?php

$keywords = array ("Baby Strollers", "Cheap Baby Strollers", "Baby Stroller Sale", "Girls Baby Strollers", "Boys Baby Strollers", "Infant Baby Strollers", "Jogging Strollers", "Two-Seat Strollers", "Jumper Seat Strollers", "Graco Baby Strollers");

$random = rand(0,9);
echo $keywords[$random];
?>
```

All I did was add the line $random = rand(0,9) and then replace the key value in the echo's array with $random.

But take a look at our random function. Notice I selected (0,9) for our random number generator. Why? Because our array index starts at zero, and goes to 9. So I want our random number to generate between 0 and 9.

Since we're working with 10 keywords in our array, an easy mistake would be to write $random = rand(1,10) but that wouldn't work.

Associative Arrays

Associative Arrays are just like Numeric Arrays except instead of using numbers for the key values, we use words (or numbers too, but usually words).

With Associative Arrays, we "Associate" the key with it's value whereas with Numeric Arrays we just assign numbers based on what position the value is in the list of values.

Here's how an Associate Array is built:

```
<?php
$variable['key'] = "value";
$variable['key2'] = "value2";
$variable['key3'] = "value3";
$variable['key4'] = "value4";
?>
```

And is called like this:

```
<?php
echo $variable['key'];
?>
```

You can see, it's a lot more work building these things, and you can't easily use our randomization trick. But I suppose it's important for you to at least know Associative Arrays exist.

Let's look at a classic example:

```
<?php

$ages['James'] = "32";
$ages['Scott'] = "30";
$ages['Kirk'] = "34";
$ages['Tina'] = "29";

echo $ages['James'];

?>
```

In this example, we've created an array of ages (32, 30, 34, and 29) and the key's are James, Scott, Kirk, and Tina. In this example, "32" would be printed to the screen.

Just be aware that Associative Arrays exist. You may need them some day. But more realistically, you'll probably stick with Numeric Arrays for basic Affiliate Marketing web work.

Functions

We're getting to the end of our PHP basic concepts; functions are the last main concept we'll be learning.

Functions are complicated, but they're here to make our lives easier.

There are two types of functions that we'll be looking at:

1. PHP's built in functions

2. Functions that we build ourselves

First of all, what is a function? Basically a function takes some input that you designate, does something to it, then returns some value.

They look like this:

```
<?php

function my_function( ) {
 Do some stuff;
```

```
 return $something;
}

?>
```

At least functions should look familiar, they should remind you of the same general format we saw when working with IF/ELSE statements and Loops.

Usually, your PHP code will load whenever someone visits your web page. But that's not necessarily the case for functions. They need to be called specifically. (though you can set them up to be called automatically when someone loads your web page).

Think of them as little side programs that run for specific purposes.

Building our own functions is really outside the scope of this book. I just want you to be aware of them. If you want to learn how to harness the awesome power of functions, you can pick up a *real* PHP programming book and read all about them.

But I do want you to be aware of PHP's built in functions because we'll use them all the time. In fact, you already HAVE used them.

The Random number generator is really just one of PHP's built in functions. It's a little program that takes in input and outputs some stuff. In this case the input is the range of numbers we give it, ie rand (1,10); the 1,10 is the input we are, well, inputting into it.

It then generates a random number, which it then outputs to us.

That's a function.

There's a lot of other useful functions that PHP comes with that you'll want to use. Things like:

- Calendar Functions
- Date Functions
- Directory Functions
- Mail Functions
- Mysql functions
- And many more...

Let's look at a couple useful ones. How about the Date function. I like to use the date function in a couple ways on my web sites, first in the copyright statement at the bottom of the page.

I can use it to put the current year, and update automatically every year so I don't have to go back through all my thousands of web sites updating the copyright year.

The other reason I use it is to put the days date at the top of the web page to make the thing seem current.

Both are done easily with the date function in PHP. Let's take a look:

```
<?php
$date=getdate(date("U"));
print("$date[weekday], $date[month] $date[mday],
$date[year]");
?>
```

That code would print out the days date in this format:

Monday, October 29, 2012

If we wanted to just print out the year for the copyright notice, we'd just have to modify that last line to look like this:

```
print("$date[year]");
```

Pretty simple.

There's just way too many built in PHP functions to go through in this book, but you can run a Google search for them if you want.

A good place to start is the list at:
http://www.w3schools.com/php/default.asp

Conclusion

So by now you should have a pretty solid foundation of basic PHP programming concepts. Congratulations for getting this far!

I've tried to trick you into thinking there wasn't much programming in this book...and that this isn't a *real* programming book.

But the truth is, if you've made it this far and understood even HALF of what we discussed in this chapter; you're well on your way to being an actual programmer.

By now, you should be able to recognize the basic structure of PHP code.

You should have a solid understanding of Variables, and a pretty good grasp on IF/THEN and IF/ELSE statements.

You should know that there are things called Loops, what they're supposed to be used for, and maybe be able to use them if you absolutely HAD to.

You should have a good grip on comparison operators so that we can do tests like figuring out if $a greater than $b.

You should be able to whip up a random number and maybe understand how to use an array.

And you should know that there are things called functions and might want to learn how to use them some day.

Now that we've got the basics behind us, let's dive in and learn a few PHP tricks that every Affiliate Marketer should have in their tool belt.

CHAPTER FOUR

PHP Tricks For Affiliate Marketers

Over the years I've build nearly 4,000 Affiliate Marketing Websites selling millions of different items.

There's simply no way to build a network of sites that large, with so many different products, without heavily using PHP for automation.

Over the years I've come up with quite a few tricks that come in handy when building Affiliate Marketing websites and I'm going to share some of the more useful ones with you in this chapter.

It's going to seem like a hodgepodge of different things that don't really have anything to do with each other... and that's exactly what it is!

This isn't a chapter that you need to read from start to finish. You can browse and read the things that you think you'll use and ignore the rest... or just read it all, it doesn't really matter.

In the next Chapter I'm going to show you how to template out an entire website so that we can customize them programmatically; automatically. We'll be using some of the tricks we learn in this chapter for that, and then expand out to an entire framework.

Let's get started!

Adding The Date To Your Pages

I mentioned earlier a way to add the date to your webpage, but there's a much easier way to do it and you can tweak this method in lots of different ways.

This is important because it's handy to put a copyright (c) notice at the bottom of your web pages and it's common to put the year after the (c) mark. And it's a huge pain to update those dates manually every year. Luckily PHP will do it for you.

Here's the basic code:

```
<?php echo date('Y'); ?>
```

That code will create this output: 2013 (or whatever the current year is). Notice the 'Y', that Y stands for year. Big leap there...

You can tweak this bit of code to output whatever kind of date you want, day, week, month, year, in lots of different formats by tweaking that Y. Here's a list of some of the more useful options, you can get the whole list at: **http://php.net/manual/en/function.date.php**

d... Day of the month, 2 digits with leading zeros 01 to 31

D... A textual representation of a day, three letters Mon through Sun

j... Day of the month without leading zeros 1 to 31

l... (lowercase 'L') | A full textual representation of the day of the week Sun - Sat

F... A full textual representation of a month, such as January or March January through December

m... Numeric representation of a month, with leading zeros 01 through 12

M... A short textual representation of a month, three letters Jan through Dec

n... Numeric representation of a month, without leading zeros 1 through 12

Y... A full numeric representation of a year, 4 digits Examples: 1999 or 2003

y... A two digit representation of a year Examples: 99 or 03

a... Lowercase Ante meridiem and Post meridiem am or pm

A... Uppercase Ante meridiem and Post meridiem AM or PM

e... Timezone identifier (added in PHP 5.1.0) Examples: UTC, GMT, Atlantic/Azores

You can mix and match those to string out longer things like current dates:

```
<?php echo date('l jS \of F, Y'); ?>
```

That would print out the day of the week, the number of the month the month, and the year like this:

Wednesday 31st of October, 2012

Notice how I put \of in there...that just print out the word "of" and the comma after the F prints out a comma.

You can slap that line of code at the top of every web page and it will display the current date in that format...which makes it seem like your web page is "current", which is fun.

You can use the day of the month in an if/then statement to show different content on even days of the month versus odd days of the month.

That's a good way to make the search engines think that your site is constantly being updated and changing.

There's just lots of fun things you can do with the date function in PHP.

Be sure to visit the PHP.net manual page for date:

http://php.net/manual/en/function.date.php

String Replace

Another handy bit of code is the string replace code. I use it ALL the time. You'll especially see me use it in the next chapter where we need to modify variables.

String Replace basically takes a variable and changes it however you designate. You can replace certain letters in the string, remove or add certain words to a string, add or remove weird things like dashes (-) or other punctuation and lots of other cool stuff.

Here's what the code looks like:

```
<?php $new_variable = str_replace("OLD", "NEW",
$old_variable); ?>
```

In that code, we start with our variable, which I've named $old_variable. str_replace searches through $old_variable looking for whatever you type in between the first set of quotation marks (where I typed OLD) and replaces it with whatever you typed between the second set of quotation marks (where I typed NEW), and then saves the output to a new variable (that I've called $new_variable).

So for instance, this line of code:

```
<?php
$variable = "John Elder is a PHP coding God";
$new_variable = str_replace("God", "Dork", $variable);
echo $new_variable;
?>
```

...will change the sentence "John Elder is a PHP coding God" to the sentence "John Elder is a PHP coding Dork".

A couple things to note. You don't have to output to a new variable. You can output to the same variable. But if you do that, the old stuff that was originally in the first variable will be copied over. ie, I could write the code as:

```
<?php
$variable = "John Elder is a PHP coding God";
$variable = str_replace("God", "Dork", $variable); ?>
```

And $variable would become "John Elder is a PHP coding Dork".

The other thing to note is that you don't have to type in words, you can use other variables instead. For instance:

```
<?php
$variable = "John Elder is a PHP coding God";
$old_word = "God";
$new_word = "Dork";
$variable = str_replace($old_word, $new_word,
$variable);
echo $variable;
?>
```

Will give you the same output: "John Elder is a PHP coding Dork".

str_replace is incredibly useful in tons of different ways. Let's say we have a link and want to make it into a keyword that we can stuff into a variable and use throughout our site. str_replace makes it easy to do that.

```
<?php
$link = "baby-strollers.html";
$link = str_replace(".html", "", $link); // strips out the
.html from the end of our variable
$link = str_replace("-", " ", $link); // strips out the dash
(-) and replaces it with a space
```

```
echo $link;
?>
```

That bit of code changes baby-strollers.html into baby strollers.

Notice a couple of things, first if we want to remove something, just type double quotes with nothing in between ("") in the second section.

The other thing to notice is when you want to add a space, you do that by typing a space between the second set of quotation marks
(" ").

I've used that lots of times, and you'll see how using that in the next chapter when we work with templates is going to be so important.

Converting To Upper Case or Lower Case

While we're on the subject of converting strings, let's talk about converting things to upper case or lower case. PHP makes it very easy.

Let's start with upper case, the code is simply:

```
<?php strtoupper($variable); ?>
```

That will convert everything in the string to Upper Case. So if your $variable is "John Elder is a PHP coding God" it will be converted to "JOHN ELDER IS A PHP CODING GOD".

But nobody likes all upper case like that! It seems like screaming. What we really want is to just change the first letter in each word to upper case. No problem, just use ucwords:

```
<?php ucwords($variable); ?>
```

That would change the $variable "John Elder is a php coding god" to "John Elder Is A Php Coding God".

And if you only wanted to change the very first letter in the string to upper case, and nothing else...you could use ucfirst:

```
<?php ucfirst($variable); ?>
```

Which would change the $variable "john elder is a php coding god" to "John elder is a php coding god".

All in all those are pretty useful commands, and there are similar commands to change things into lower case; for instance, strtolower:

```
<?php strtolower($variable); ?>
```

Would change our $variable "John Elder Is A PHP Coding God" to "john elder is a php coding god" changing all the letters of the string to lower case.

And to change just the very first character of a string to lower case, use lcfirst:

```
<?php lcfirst($variable); ?>
```

Would change the $variable "John Elder Is a PHP Coding God" to "john Elder Is a PHP Coding God" (just the first j gets changed).

These little bits of code can really come in handy when you're trying to make sets of keywords look good.

Server Header Codes

It's handy to be able to take a URL and strip out the domain name and other information from it.

One place I like to do that is in the copyright declaration at the bottom of all my web sites.

Check out this line of code:

```
<?php echo $_SERVER['HTTP_HOST']; ?>
```

What that does is echo the domain name. So if the page is http://www.JohnElder.org/I-like-cheese.html then that line of code will echo out JohnElder.org

I like to couple that line of code with the date code we talked about earlier and slap it in the footer section of all my web sites like this:

```
Copyright (c) <?php echo date('Y'); ?> <?php echo $_SERVER['HTTP_HOST']; ?> - All Rights Reserved
```

That would echo out this:

Copyright (c) 2013 JohnElder.org - All Rights Reserved

This isn't a ground breaking piece of code or anything, but it's certainly handy when building templates that you want to scale out to thousands of sites.

Using that line of code in your template means you don't have to go in there by hand and tweak each web site on each domain name, and it's also useful because the date will update automatically every year.

Another handy server header type thing is 'REQUEST_URI' which is used like this:

```
<?php echo $_SERVER['REQUEST_URI']; ?>
```

Which will return the name of the file that you're currently looking at. For instance, if you were viewing the web page:

http://www.johnelder.org/i-like-cheese.html

...then that line of code would return /i-like-cheese.html

if you wanted to strip out the .html and the dashes, you could use the str_replace function we talked about earlier.

In fact, let's do that:

```
<?php
$variable = $_SERVER['REQUEST_URI'];
$variable = str_replace(".html", "", $variable);
$variable = str_replace("/", "", $variable);
$variable = str_replace("-", " ", $variable);
echo $variable;
?>
```

That would return "i like cheese" (without the quotes) if we were visiting the URL http://www.JohnElder.org/i-like-cheese.html

That can be very handy as we'll see later on when we get into templating websites.

One thing to keep in mind when you use REQUEST_URI, it returns the entire path. So if you're sitting in a directory, it will return the directory as well as the file name.

So for instance, if we were at:
http://www.JohnElder.org/cheese/i-like-cheese.html

...and we called REQUEST_URI, it would return:

/cheese/i-like-cheese.html

(notice the /cheese/) so keep that in mind!

Rotating Links

Whenever I build an affiliate website, one of the first things I do is research to find the major brands within that niche. I make a list of them, and then I create a page dedicated to each brand.

I put company information, a little corporate history, and maybe a short discussion on some of the major products that brand is famous for.

Depending on the niche I'm working with, I might have anywhere from 20 to 100 brand pages and I want to put links to those brand pages on all the other pages of my site.

But I don't want a list of 100 links cluttering up each page. So I break them down into lists of 10 to 20 links and then randomly show just one bunch of lists per page.

When someone reloads the page, or visits another page of my site, a new bunch of links gets shown.

The reason I do it randomly, is because the major search engines, especially Google, like to see "freshness" on a web page. ie they like to see constantly updated content.

No one can constantly update content at scale, so the next best thing is to make it LOOK like your pages are constantly updating. One of the ways I do that is with this randomly updating link list script.

It's pretty simple. All you have to do is segregate your links into lists of 10 or 20 links (or however many you want), assign those segregated lists to a variable, then call the random function that we learned earlier.

Let's pretend we're building a Baby Stroller website. Here's the 20 brand names I want to use (I'd use more but for the sake of example I'm going to keep it at 20):

4moms
Baby Buddy
Baby Jogger
Baby Trend
Badger Basket
BOB
Britax USA
BuggyGuard
Chicco
Comfy Baby
Contours
Cosco
Diono
Disney
Dream On Me
Eddie Bauer

ERGObaby
Evenflo
Graco
UPPAbaby

The first thing to do is convert them into links and assign them into groups. I'll use groups of five links each:

```
<?php
$links1 = '
<a href="4moms.html">4 Moms</a><br/>
<a href="Baby Buddy.html">Baby Buddy</a><br/>
<a href="Baby-Jogger.html">Baby Jogger</a><br/>
<a href="Baby-Trend.html">Baby Trend</a><br/>
<a href="Badger-Basket.html">Badger Basket</a><br/>';

$links2 = '
<a href="BOB.html">BOB</a><br/>
<a href="Britax-USA.html">Britax USA</a><br/>
<a href="BuggyGuard.html">Buggy Guard</a><br/>
<a href="Chicco.html">Chicco</a><br/>
<a href="Comfy-Baby.html">Comfy Baby</a><br/>';

$links3 = '
<a href="Contours.html">Contours</a><br/>
<a href="Cosco.html">Cosco</a><br/>
<a href="Diono.html">Diono</a><br/>
<a href="Disney.html">Disney</a><br/>
```

```
<a href="Dream-On-Me.html">Dream on Me</a><br/>';

$links4 = '
<a href="Eddie-Bauer.html">Eddie Bauer</a><br/>
<a href="ERGObaby.html">Ergo Baby</a><br/>
<a href="Evenflo.html">Evenflo</a><br/>
<a href="Graco.html">Graco</a><br/>
<a href="UPPAbaby.html">UPPABaby</a><br/>';

?>
```

So now we have four variable, $links1 $links2 $links3 and $links4,
All we have to do is set up a little randomization:

```
<?php
$randlinks = rand(1, 4);
if ($randlinks == 1) {echo $links1;}
if ($randlinks == 2) {echo $links2;}
if ($randlinks == 3) {echo $links3;}
if ($randlinks == 4) {echo $links4;}
?>
```

That's really all there is to it! Putting it all together, it looks like this:

```
<?php
```

```
$links1 = '
<a href="4moms.html">4 Moms</a><br/>
<a href="Baby Buddy.html">Baby Buddy</a><br/>
<a href="Baby-Jogger.html">Baby Jogger</a><br/>
<a href="Baby-Trend.html">Baby Trend</a><br/>
<a href="Badger-Basket.html">Badger Basket</a><br/>';

$links2 = '
<a href="BOB.html">BOB</a><br/>
<a href="Britax-USA.html">Britax USA</a><br/>
<a href="BuggyGuard.html">Buggy Guard</a><br/>
<a href="Chicco.html">Chicco</a><br/>
<a href="Comfy-Baby.html">Comfy Baby</a><br/>';

$links3 = '
<a href="Contours.html">Contours</a><br/>
<a href="Cosco.html">Cosco</a><br/>
<a href="Diono.html">Diono</a><br/>
<a href="Disney.html">Disney</a><br/>
<a href="Dream-On-Me.html">Dream on Me</a><br/>';

$links4 = '
<a href="Eddie-Bauer.html">Eddie Bauer</a><br/>
<a href="ERGObaby.html">Ergo Baby</a><br/>
<a href="Evenflo.html">Evenflo</a><br/>
<a href="Graco.html">Graco</a><br/>
<a href="UPPAbaby.html">UPPABaby</a><br/>';

$randlinks = rand(1, 4);
if ($randlinks == 1) {echo $links1;}
if ($randlinks == 2) {echo $links2;}
```

```
if ($randlinks == 3) {echo $links3;}
if ($randlinks == 4) {echo $links4;}
?>
```

You can add that whole snippet of code to each web page you own, but that's a little overkill.

You can also put that whole snippet of code in a separate file. Let's call it links.php.

Then, whenever you want to add your random list of links to a specific webpage, you just need to add this line of code:

```
<?php require_once('links.php'); ?>
```

The require_once command is incredibly useful, and I'll talk about it in greater detail in the next chapter. In fact, this is a great way to segue into the next chapter...

Conclusion

These are just a few snippets of PHP code that make my life as an Affiliate Marketer easier.

This list is by no means exhaustive, there are lots of other ways you can use PHP to automate things on your Affiliate Marketing web sites...

But hopefully I've given you enough to get your appetite wet. Next we'll move on to the more comprehensive part of the book where I'll walk you through templating web sites and scaling them out by actually creating a working (though terribly basic) affiliate marketing web site.

It'll be a Baby Strollers website...exciting!

CHAPTER FIVE

Templating Websites For Scale

Alright, now we're getting to the really good stuff.

If you've been an Affiliate Marketer for a while you know there's really two strategies to live by. Narrow or Broad.

Either you can focus on something very *Narrowly*...like one product or one line of product and focus on it intently, driving all your efforts into getting traffic for that one thing...

Or you can focus *Broadly* on tons of stuff; ie cast a large net and see what sticks. I tend to take the broad approach.

Why?

Because I like to let people tell me what they want, and then provide it to them. Narrow Affiliate Marketers think they know what people should want and they focus on giving it to them.

They may be right...often they aren't.

The Narrow path is expensive. You can't expect much free SEO traffic when you're selling something narrowly. Why? Because there are only so many people searching for that thing at the search engines.

If you're lucky, you might get a percentage of those searchers. But its capped. And if you have strong competitors then it's even harder to carve yourself a slice of that search engine traffic.

I take the complete opposite approach, building very broad websites that sell EVERYTHING. Then I sit back and see what the search engines find appealing by what free traffic they send me.

We call this the LongTail Keyword Approach.

Let's take an example. The keyword "Lawn Mower" gets searched for 1.5 million times every month. That sort of keyword is going to be MASSIVELY competitive to rank your website under.

Chances are you won't get any free search engine traffic from people searching for that phrase at Google.

On the other hand, the phrase "John Deere Riding Mowers Attachments" gets searched for 260 times per month. There's a very good chance that I could get a percentage of those searchers every month.

"John Deere Riding Mowers Attachments" is a long tail keyword.

There is a down side though...260 isn't enough site visitors to make any money. I might only nab 10 of those 260 searchers and get them to visit my site.

You can't make a living building affiliate marketing websites with such low traffic.

The solution is simple. You need to target MILLIONS of those long tail keywords. That means you need web sites that have MILLIONS of pages...one web page for each long tail keyword.

If you're sneaky, PHP gives you the tools to do that.

The next problem is that it's impossible to build web sites with MILLIONS of web pages by hand. It would take you your whole life to build one site... and chances are, you're going to want to own more than one website (I currently own about 4,000).

So we need to automate the creation of your web sites....and that means templating them out.

What's a template?

You know what a template is...it's a...well...template. Its the framework of a website that's basically identical so that you can deploy it over and over.

The template is the same...the page structure is the same...the layout is the same...but we'll use a little PHP to automatically tweak each template to make it look unique.

PHP gives us lots of tools to do just that. But first, we need to build the template.

Still not quite with me?

Think of Amazon.com

Most of the pages on Amazon are completely identical....the only difference is that the item for sale on each page is different. But the pages all have the same structure, the same layout, etc.

There's a picture of the product at the top of the page, along with pricing information, followed by product information, followed by a list of customer reviews.

On the left hand side of the screen is a list of links to browse related categories, on the right hand side of the screen is a "buy it now" button that you can click on to buy whatever the thing is.

Amazon sells millions of products. Do you think some designer created each of those pages by hand? Of course not. They built one template and then built it to automatically customize for each item.

We're going to do something similar. We're going to build a simple template that auto-updates based on the products you're going to want to sell as an Affiliate Marketer.

Download the Files

I'm going to walk you through the code right here, but I'll also post the files online at my website so that you can download them and see them in action, or use them yourself.

You can see them at **http://www.JohnElder.org/phpbook/templates/files.zip**

As we go through this, I'll point you to specific files there that you can check out.

Getting Started

First things first, let's map out this project. We're going to build a simple Affiliate Marketing website template that shows an adsense ad, followed by some affiliate product listings.

To start, let's build our initial index.php file (index.php is usually the file you start with).

The goal of templating is to be able to centralize all the moving parts of the web site into just a few files. So if you need to change something on all the millions of pages of products, you can make a change to just one or two files and those changes will automatically propagate throughout the entire site.

You'll understand what I'm talking about more as we go on.

The first thing we need to do is talk about the REQUIRE_ONCE PHP command. It looks like this:

```
<?php require_once('file.php'); ?>
```

What does that simple line of code do? It pulls whatever is sitting in the file.php file, and echo's it onto the current page. BTW, you'll replace file.php with whatever the file you want to include is named.

Why is that line so important? Templating....

Let's start by breaking down the index.php file into sections. We'll break each section down and make a file out of it, and add it to our index.php file by using the require_once command.

Here's a boxy version of the page we want to build:

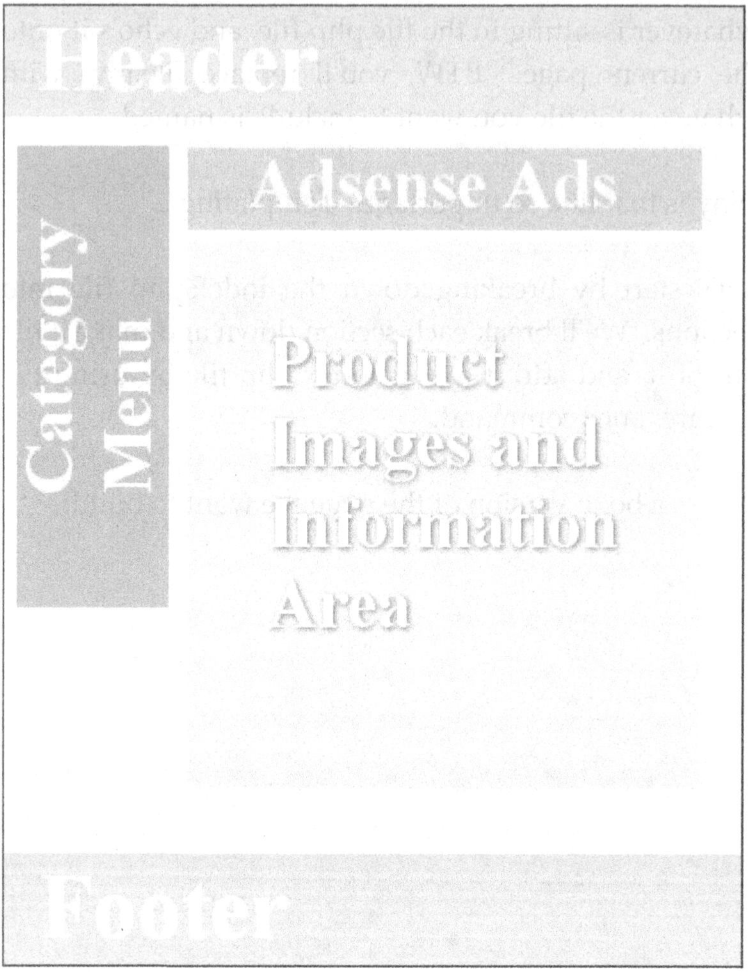
Header
Category Menu
Adsense Ads
Product Images and Information Area
Footer

Alright, granted - this is a very basic layout but I want to keep it basic while I show you how to break web sites up into templates. So bear with me.

This page is broken up into 5 main sections:

- Header Section

- Left Menu Section

- Adsense Ad Section

- Product Info Section

- Footer Section

We'll create a separate file for each of them. Let's call the files:

header.php

left_menu.php

adsense_ads.php

products.php

footer.php

In each of those files we'll place the code that will be used to create each section in our index.php file. For now we'll just type the word that it is; ie we'll type header in the header.php file, type footer in the footer.php file, etc.

So let's build our index.php file. It's a template...so it's going to be pretty easy to build. Here we go:

```
<!DOCTYPE html>
<html>
 <head>
 <title>Our Affiliate Marketing Web Page</title>
 </head>
 <body>

  <?php require_once('header.php'); ?>
  <br/>
  <?php require_once('left_menu.php'); ?>
  <br/>
  <?php require_once('adsense_ads.php'); ?>
  </br>
  <?php require_once('products.php'); ?>
  <br/>
  <?php require_once('footer.php'); ?>

 </body>
</html>
```

Right now we don't have anything in the various files that we're "require_once"-ing except the words we just typed in, so our index page will look like this:

So let's create the HTML code for what our page will eventually look like, then I'll break up that code and put each piece in its respective file.

The first thing we're going to need to do is create a CSS stylesheet file, I'll name it style.css and put a reference to it on our index.php page in the header section.

```
<!DOCTYPE html>
<html>
 <head>
<link href="style.css" rel="stylesheet">
<title>Our Affiliate Marketing Web Page</title>
 </head>
 <body>

<div id="maincontainer">
```

```
<div id="topsection">

<div class="innertube">
<h1>Our Product</h1>
</div>
</div>

<div id="contentwrapper">
<div id="contentcolumn">

<div id="adsense_ads">
Adsense Ads Go here
</div>

<div class="innertube">

Product Information
</div>
</div>
</div>

<div id="leftcolumn">
<div class="innertube">
<ul>
<li>Category 1</li>
<li>Category 2</li>
<li>Category 3</li>
<li>Category 4</li>
<li>Category 5</li>
</ul>
</div>
```

```
</div>

<div id="footer">
Copyright &copy; <?php echo date('Y'); ?> <?php echo
$_SERVER['HTTP_HOST'];    ?>    -    All    Rights
Reserved</div>
</body>
</html>
```

Now let's build our simple style.css stylesheet. Right now there's not much to it, we just need to write CSS for the few div's we created in our html above:

```
body {
 margin:0;
 padding:0;
 line-height: 1.5em;
 margin-top:10px;
}

#maincontainer {
 width: 840px; /*Width of main container*/
 margin: 0 auto; /*Center container on page*/
 border-color: #404040;
 border-style: solid;
 border-width: 1px;
}

#topsection {
```

```
 background: #E2E2E2;
 height: 90px; /*Height of top section*/
}

#topsection h1 {
 margin: 0;
 padding-top: 25px;
}

#adsense_ads {
  background: #FFC0FF;
  width: 500px;
  height: 80px;
  margin-top:10px;
  margin-left: 10px;



}



#contentwrapper {
 float: left;
 width: 100%;
}

#contentcolumn {
 margin-left: 210px; /*Set left margin to
LeftColumnWidth*/
}

#leftcolumn {
```

```
float: left;
width: 200px; /*Width of left column*/
margin-left: -830px; /*Set left margin to -(MainContainerWidth)*/
margin-top: 10px;
background: #C0C0FF;
}

#footer {
clear: left;
width: 100%;
background: #E2E2E2;
color: black;
text-align: center;
padding: 4px 0;
}


.innertube {
margin: 10px; /*Margins for inner DIV inside each column (to provide padding)*/
margin-top: 0;
}
```

So that's going to give us a webpage that looks pretty much like our original site layout:

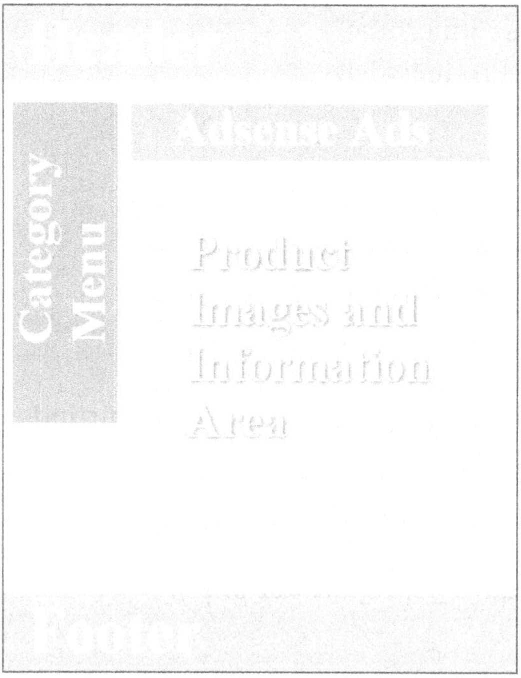

Or close enough for now. Next we need to chop apart the HTML from our index.php and put each section in its appropriate file ie the header code goes into the header.php file, the footer code goes into the footer.php file, etc.

So let's start with the header stuff. Place the following code into your header.php file:

```
<div id="maincontainer">
```

```
<div id="topsection">
<div class="innertube">
<h1>Our Product</h1>
</div>
</div>

<div id="contentwrapper">
<div id="contentcolumn">
```

And be sure to replace that code in our index.html file with this line:

```
<?php require_once('header.php'); ?>
```

Next we want to stick this code into our adsense_ads.php file:

```
<div id="adsense_ads">
Adsense Ads Go here
</div>
```

And replace it with this line of code in index.php

```
<?php require_once('adsense_ads.php'); ?>
```

Next we need to add this code to our products.php file:

```
<div class="innertube">
Product Information
<br/><br/><br/><br/><br/><br/>
</div>
</div>
</div>
```

And be sure to replace it with this line in the index.php file:

```
<?php require_once('products.php'); ?>
```

Next we need to add this code into the left_menu.php file:

```
<div id="leftcolumn">
<div class="innertube">
<ul>
<li>Category 1</li>
<li>Category 2</li>
<li>Category 3</li>
<li>Category 4</li>
<li>Category 5</li>
</ul>
```

```
</div>
</div>
```

And be sure to replace it with this line in your index.php file:

```
<?php require_once('left_menu.php'); ?>
```

Finally, we need to add this code to your footer.php file:

```
<div id="footer">
Copyright &copy; <?php echo date('Y'); ?> <?php echo
$_SERVER['HTTP_HOST']; ?> - All Rights
Reserved</div>
```

And be sure to replace it with this line in your index.php file:

```
<?php require_once('footer.php'); ?>
```

So now we've got each section of our main index.php page segregated into its own separate php file (header.php, footer.php, left_menu.php, adsense_ads.php, and products.php).

Our index page should now look like this:

```
<!DOCTYPE html>
<html>
 <head>
<link href="style.css" rel="stylesheet">
<title>Our Affiliate Marketing Web Page</title>
 </head>
 <body>

<?php require_once('header.php'); ?>

<?php require_once('adsense_ads.php'); ?>

<?php require_once('products.php'); ?>

<?php require_once('left_menu.php'); ?>

<?php require_once('footer.php'); ?>

</body>
</html>
```

Ok, so that's pretty straight forward. The HTML and CSS code and site design really isn't important here, what's important is the concept of separating different sections of a web page and splitting them up into their own php file and then including them with the use of our require_once php command.

Let's Customize Things Now...

Before we move on into the more advanced topic of scaling this website, let's clean things up a little and make it look more like a real website.

Let's make it into a Baby Stroller web site.

The first thing we need to do is create a variables.php file to hold some variables. For now I'll just put this code in it:

```
<?php

$main_keyword = "Baby Strollers";

?>
```

Now we need to add this line of code into our index.php right at the very top of the file:

```
<?php include('variables.php'); ?>
```

What that line of code does is tell our webpage to include the stuff that's sitting in our variables.php file. In this case, the only thing that's sitting in there is a variable called $main_keyword that's set to "Baby Strollers". But now, whenever I want to use the phrase "Baby Strollers" in our index.php file, I can just type this line of code in:

```
<?php echo $main_keyword; ?>
```

In fact, let's do that right now. I'll update the index.php file to include that line where the Title tag now says "Our Affiliate Marketing Web Page".

I'll also add it to our products.php page, replacing the "Product Information" line of text with <?php echo $main_keyword; ?>.

And while we're at it, let's update the header.php file the same way.

The next thing I want to do is drop in our adsense code into the adsense_ad.php file.

Finally let's create some category links in the "left_menu.php" file to replace the category 1, category 2, etc that's already sitting there. I'll just grab some common Baby stroller brand names for these.

Now we're getting somewhere, but it's not enough. Here's what it looks like so far:

Let's get some content going here. After all, you can't have an affiliate website without some affiliate listings.

There are a zillion ways to add affiliate products for sale on any given webpage. Personally I like to use the API version of a program called **PHPZon** **http://www.marketingfool.com/phpzonrocks.html**

What it does is show Amazon listings based on whatever keyword you feed it. It costs a few bucks to buy the program, but you can use it over and over on as many websites as you like.

It's beyond the scope of this book to teach you the inner workings of PHPZon, and since you can't use it without buying it, I'm going to use something else for our test site here today.

Instead I'm going to add a Shopzilla widget. If you aren't a shopzilla affiliate, I suggest you sign up, it's free.

So let's add this bit of Shopzilla widget code to our products.php file:

```
<div style="position:relative; border:1px solid #aaa;
font-family:helvetica,tahoma,arial,sans-serif; color:#333;
width:480px; height:730px;"><iframe width="480px"
height="690px" frameborder="0" scrolling="no"
src="http://widgets.bizrate.com/Bizrate-
ProductSearch/content.html?publisherId=46473&catego
ryId=0&keyword=<?php echo $main_keyword;
?>&col=3&row=3&placementid=1"></iframe><div
style="position:absolute; left:0; bottom:0; font-size:11px;
width:100%; height:40px; color:#403D35;"><img
src="http://adserve.shopzilla.com/img/publisherID-
46473/assetID-2772/placementID-1/" /></div></div>
```

Notice how I put <?php echo $main_keyword; ?> in there next to the keyword= thing?

So here's what we've got so far:

...Which is pretty good for a very basic website. Next we're going to dive into some really advanced topics that will show you how to really scale this thing into millions of pages.

Scaling Our Web Site

So we've got a basic affiliate marketing webpage, but it's just ONE page. What we really need is to scale this sucker into the millions of pages region.

That's what I'm going to teach you in this section.

First things first, create a new file called fun.php

In that page copy the exact contents of our index.php file. Just copy and paste it in there:

```
<?php include('variables.php'); ?>
<!DOCTYPE html>
<html>
 <head>
<link href="style.css" rel="stylesheet">
<title><?php echo $main_keyword; ?></title>
 </head>
 <body>

<?php require_once('header.php'); ?>

<?php require_once('adsense_ads.php'); ?>

<?php require_once('products.php'); ?>
```

```
<?php require_once('left_menu.php'); ?>

<?php require_once('footer.php'); ?>

</body>
</html>
```

Now create a new file and name it .htaccess

.htaccess files freak people out a little bit because they aren't named like other files (like index.php or products.php or sale.html or whatever).

It's ok, it's not a typo... name it .htaccess and put these lines of code in it:

```
<IfModule mod_rewrite.c>
RewriteEngine On
RewriteBase /
RewriteCond %{REQUEST_FILENAME} !-s
RewriteRule ^([a-zA-Z0-9_-]+.html)$
fun.php?keyword=$1 [L]
RewriteRule ^([a-zA-Z0-9_-]+.html)/$
fun.php?keyword=$1 [L]

RewriteRule ^(.*)\.html$ $1.php
[T=application/x-httpd-php,L]
</IfModule>
```

What exactly does all that mean? You don't really need to know; but if you're curious...

The first chunk of code tells the web server to take any URL we type into our web browser and instead direct the user to our newly created fun.php file...

But not to change the text that's in the browser bar on the browser...

So if someone types in http://yoursite.com/baby-strollers.html into their browser, our webserver will show the page fun.php instead.

It'll make more sense in a bit.

The second bit of code instructs the server to show .php file extensions as .html file extensions now.

So what's the point of this? With just one file "fun.php" we can now create millions of pages simply by creating a list of them.

Try it out...head to:

http://www.JohnElder.org/phpbook/templates/baby-strollers.html

or

http://www.JohnElder.org/phpbook/templates/lawn-mowers.html

or

anything else you like. Just type in anything after:

http://www.JohnElder.org/phpbook/templates/

and stick a .html at the end, and that page will pop up (but its really just our masked fun.php file!).

Now we need to tweak our fun.php file to autogenerate content based on the name of the file that gets called.

For instance, if someone types in lawn-mowers.html into the browser (or follows a link there or whatever) we want the fun.php page to realize on its own that the person is looking for lawn mower information, and show it some.

This is easier than it seems. Just add these lines to the top of our fun.php file:

```
<?php $_SERVER['QUERY_STRING'];
$item = str_replace("-", " ", $_GET['keyword']);
$item = str_replace(".html", "", $item);
$item = ucwords ($item);
?>
```

What that code does is look at the Query String (the URL that get's typed into a web browser) and strips out the last file name from the URL and assigns it to the variable $item.

So now we can use the $item variable in our products.php file in the shopzilla code. Replace the $main_keyword variable with our new $item variable. products.php will now look like this:

```
<div class="innertube">
<br/><center>
<div style="position:relative; border:1px solid #aaa;
font-family:helvetica,tahoma,arial,sans-serif; color:#333;
width:480px; height:730px;"><iframe width="480px"
height="690px" frameborder="0" scrolling="no"
src="http://widgets.bizrate.com/Bizrate-
ProductSearch/content.html?publisherId=46473&catego
ryId=0&keyword=<?php echo $item;
?>&col=3&row=3&placementid=1"></iframe><div
style="position:absolute; left:0; bottom:0; font-size:11px;
width:100%; height:40px; color:#403D35;"><img
src="http://adserve.shopzilla.com/img/publisherID-
46473/assetID-2772/placementID-1/" /></div></div>
<br/>
</center>
</div>
</div>
</div>
```

We also need to add this line of code to the top of our index.php file so that it doesn't get left behind:

```
<?php $item = $main_keyword ?>
```

Just add that to the second line in our index.php file.

So now we have a website that has potentially millions of web pages. But none of those pages exists until someone visits them either by following a link or by typing in an URL into their web browser.

Luckily Google will help us out. See, Google spiders a web site and follows all the links that it finds. So we just need to automatically generate a list of millions of potential pages for our site, and let Google do the rest.

Google will crawl from link to link and when it does it will add those "pages" into its index. Then when someone see's a link to one of those pages at Google and clicks the link, our web server will create that page on the fly by directing them to our fun.php page which will modify itself to show shopzilla ads based on the URL the person is visiting.

But before we do that, we need to clean up the left hand menu. Right now it just has like 5 bullet points that don't do anything.

Cleaning Up The Left Hand Menu

So let's replace those useless bullet points with links to pages of our site. Instead of:

Baby Jogger
Bugaboo
Peg Perego
Maclaren
UppAbaby

Let's change them to:

Baby-Jogger.html
Bugaboo.html
Peg-Perego.html
Maclaren.html
UppAbaby.html

...and make them into links. So here's what our new left_menu.php file should look like:

```
<div id="leftcolumn">
<div class="innertube">
```

```
<ul>
<li><a href="Baby-Jogger.html">Baby Jogger</a></li>
<li><a href="Bugaboo.html">Bugaboo</a></li>
<li><a href="Peg-Perego.html">Peg Perego</a></li>
<li><a href="Maclaren.html">Maclaren Strollers</a></li>
<li><a href="UppAbaby.html">UppaBaby Strollers</a></li>
</ul>
</div>
</div>
```

Now let's add a quick line of code to our header.php file to add a little more content. Add this line directly below the closing </h1> tag:

```
<?php echo $item; ?>
```

That will just print out our $item variable directly below our main Baby Stroller header.

Now the only thing left is to autogenerate a zillion links to pages within our own website. There are countless ways to do that, and you may want to just think about it and use your imagination.

Basically you just need some way to autogenerate related keywords. So if someone visits your jogger-stroller.html page, you need to autogenerate keywords related to jogger-strollers and then format them into links at the bottom of your page.

The formatting keywords into links is pretty simple with php, the autogenerating the keywords is a little trickier.

I talk about different methods to do this at my MarketingFool.com website and especially (in more detail) at my insiders.MarketingFool.com members-only website. I highly suggest you check into both those resources.

Personally I like to use a program called **PHPBay** which is made by the same people that make PHPZon. I use the api version to generate links, and you need to configure the output file a little to make this work, and it's not free...but it's totally worth it.

Basically we'll just add this line of code to our products.php file directly under the shopzilla code:

```
<?php
include_once("phpbay/ebay.php");
phpBayAPI("$item", 10);
?>
```

That code won't mean anything to you, it's just a call to the PHPBay api. One thing to notice, see how I put $item and 10 in there? That tells phpBay what to search for (our $item keyword) and how many results to return (10).

PHPBay returns eBay listings. Pictures, information, and links to click on to buy the items shown directly on eBay. We're not using it for that though.

We're just stripping out all the junk (the pictures of items, info about them, links, etc) and leaving the item titles. Then formatting those titles into links.

You do that by modifying the template.ebay.results.html file. Erase everything that's in there and replace it with this:

```
<li><a href="%%link_url%%">%%title%%</a></li>
```

The template.ebay.results.html file is located in the directory: /phpbay/templates/ that comes with PHPBay.

So what have we done here? Now there's 10 links at the bottom of each page of our website. And if you click on any of those links, there are 10 different links, and if you click on any of those links...and on and on infinitely.

Google will visit your website, see those links, and start crawling. Each page will be generated on the fly when Google crawls them (even though it will always just be our fun.php page getting shown with new content based on that pages actual $item variable that's generated by the URL).

In no time you could have hundreds of thousands of "pages" indexed at Google. Then when they show up in search results and people click on them...walla.

That's all there is to templating and scaling a website.

You can download all the completed files that I used in this chapter at:
http://www.JohnElder.org/phpbook/templates/files.zip

And you can see the site we just built in action at:
http://www.JohnElder.org/phpbook/templates/index.php

Granted this was a pretty lame looking Affiliate website, but I hope it at least showed you the basic concepts of splitting a site up into sections and then scaling it with my handy .htaccess trick.

If you're interested in learning how I build more complex affiliate web sites, check out my Members-Only Insiders group at:

http://insiders.marketingfool.com

...where I show how to build thick and thin niche sites, portal sites, shopping sites, price comparison sites, and much more. Membership isn't free, but I don't charge an arm and a leg like a lot of Internet Marketing guru's out there.

Check the Appendix of this book for a special deep discount on membership. It's my thanks to you for buying this book.

Here's a picture of our final affiliate website:

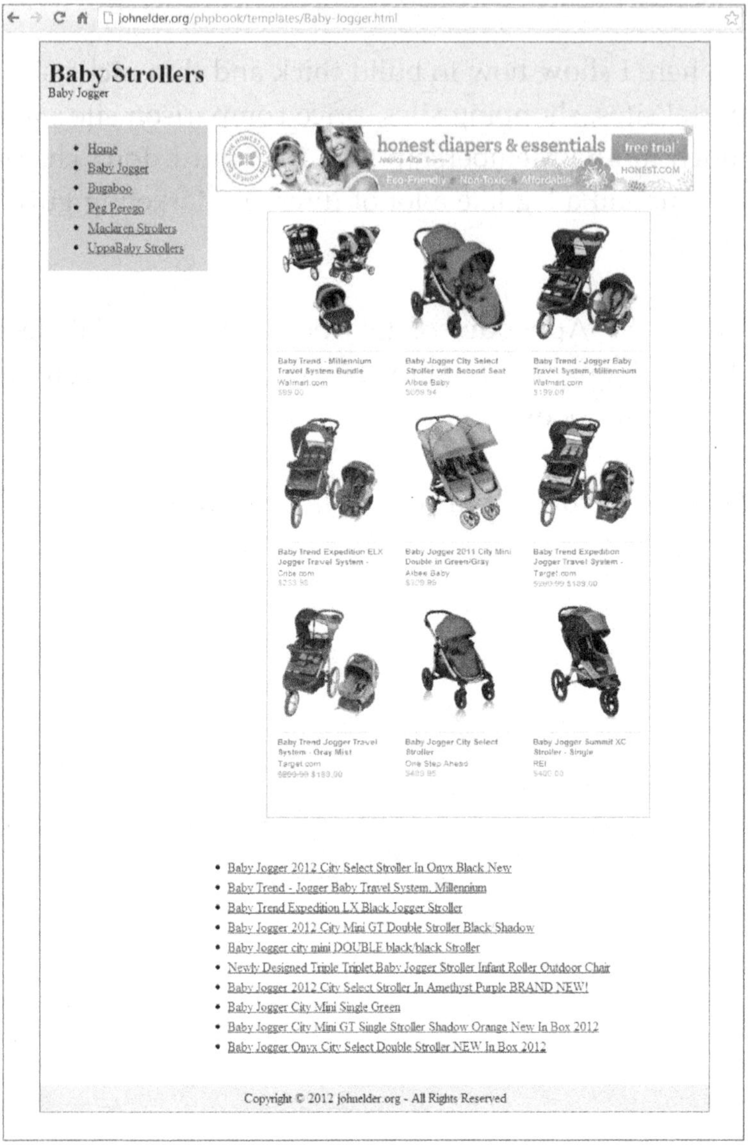
johnelder.org/phpbook/templates/Baby-Jogger.html
Baby Strollers
Baby Jogger
Home
Baby Jogger
Bugaboo
Peg Perego
Maclaren Strollers
UppaBaby Strollers
honest diapers & essentials
free trial
HONEST.COM
Eco-Friendly
Non-Toxic
Affordable
Baby Jogger 2012 City Select Stroller In Onyx Black New
Baby Trend - Jogger Baby Travel System, Millennium
Baby Trend Expedition LX Black Jogger Stroller
Baby Jogger 2012 City Mini GT Double Stroller Black Shadow
Baby Jogger city mini DOUBLE black/black Stroller
Newly Designed Triple Triplet Baby Jogger Stroller Infant Roller Outdoor Chair
Baby Jogger 2012 City Select Stroller In Amethyst Purple BRAND NEW!
Baby Jogger City Mini Single Green
Baby Jogger City Mini GT Single Stroller Shadow Orange New In Box 2012
Baby Jogger Onyx City Select Double Stroller NEW In Box 2012
Copyright © 2012 johnelder.org - All Rights Reserved

CHAPTER SIX

Webpage Text Spinning

What is text spinning?

Spinning takes a set of words, sentences, or paragraphs and shuffles them based on some sort of pre-set criteria, usually randomly.

Traditionally people use software to take a written article and create hundreds of spun articles out of them. They then use the many differently spun articles for article marketing purposes, and for seo purposes.

What do I mean by spun? Let's take a sentence:

The cat is really ugly.

You can spin that sentence a zillion ways by changing a few words and all the different sentences will basically mean the same thing. Let's break apart that sentence into each of it's separate words:

The
cat
is
really
ugly

To spin that sentence, we need to come up with synonyms for each of those words. Here's some examples:

The: A, Our, My, Their, His, Her, Bob's

cat: kitty, kitty cat, kitten, feline, pussy cat

is: was, is always, has been, is usually

really: truly, quite, extremely, totally

ugly: hideous, ugly looking, unsightly, unattractive

Ok, some of those aren't exactly synonyms, but you get the picture. We could randomly use any of those words instead of it's original word, and the sentence will basically mean the same thing.

Try it out, randomly select any word from the list and re-construct the sentence:

"Our kitty is usually quite hideous."

Compare it to our original:

"The cat is really ugly."

Not exactly the same, but both those sentences basically convey the same thought.

Why is this important for us as affiliate marketers?

We learned earlier how to template out a web site in order to create millions of pages. If Google see's the exact same content on every single one of our pages, with the only difference being some different ads on each page, they might determine that we have a low-quality website and give us a terrible ranking in their search engine...or ban us altogether.

So we need to make each page as unique as possible, yet still automate the process as much as possible. Spinning helps us do that.

Now before we go on, I must warn you...

I went back and forth with myself on whether or not to add this chapter to the book at all.

Why? Because spinning text on a webpage is controversial. Some people, including Google, view it as a blackhat method. Others see it as more of a gray area.

Personally I think spinning is like any other tool out there. It's not inherently good or bad, it just depends on how you use it.

If you're using it to trick Google into indexing pages that don't really offer any usefulness to the average site visitor just to get a better search engine ranking, then I think that's bad.

If you're using it to tweak your websites to gain better search engine placement, but at the same time using it in a way that's useful to your site visitors (or at least not detrimental to them) then I don't see anything wrong with it at all.

Google...

In the past I would create websites with one article, and spin it millions of times...thus creating millions of pages.

Google used to love that. They viewed each of those pages as unique, even though they were basically the same article spun over and over.

While it worked, it worked well and I was able to use that technique to get millions of my web pages indexed at Google, gaining a mountain of free long tail keyword traffic that translated into adsense clicks and affiliate product buys on a massive scale.

But Google eventually figured out how to detect when a page is filled with mostly spun content and stopped indexing those sites of mine.

Now I only use spinning very sparsely, and for certain circumstances.

Google is a fickle beast though; what works today won't work tomorrow, but will sometimes work next week. And that's why I've decided to add this chapter on spinning.

Spin Text

Before we get into the PHP behind spinning, we need to discuss spin text. Spin text is the format you use to designate which words you want to spin, and in what manner.

There are lots of different spin text formats, but most will basically look something like this:

```
{{word 1|word 2|word 3|word 4|word 5}}
```

Notice how each word in the set is separated by | the pipe symbol. When spun, any of those 5 words will be selected randomly and shown.

So let's stick with our previous example. The spin text for that set of words would look something like this:

{{The|A|Our|My|Their|His|Her|Bob's}}{{cat|kitty|kitty cat|kitten|feline|pussy cat}} {{is|was|is always|has been|is usually}}
{{really|truly|quite|extremely|totally}}
{{ugly|hideous|ugly looking|unsightly|unattractive}}

It's a very simple and short sentence, but already it's becoming hard to read. That's why many people use software to generate and manage their spin text.

I use something called "The Best Spinner"
http://www.marketingfool.com/bestspinnerrocks.html

Most would agree that it's the industry standard in spinning software. I highly recommend you check it out.

But now that we have our spin text, we need to write some PHP code to spin it on a web page.

Spinning Text With PHP

First things first, we need to modify that spin text to parse out any characters that will give our PHP code problems. Usually this means quotation marks and things like that.

Take a look through our list of words. See anything that might give us some trouble?

"Bob's" has an apostrophe and that will throw off PHP, so we need to "escape" out the apostrophe. Do that by sticking a backslash in front of it in our spin text, like this: Bob\'s

Our spin text will now look like this:

{{The|A|Our|My|Their|His|Her|Bob\'s}}{{cat|kitty|k itty cat|kitten|feline|pussy cat}} {{is|was|is always|has been|is usually}} {{really|truly|quite|extremely|totally}} {{ugly|hideous|ugly looking|unsightly|unattractive}}

Next we need to add our PHP code, basically we'll be wrapping out spin text into a variable:

```
<?php
include ('spin.php');
$string =
'{{The|A|Our|My|Their|His|Her|Bob\'s}}{{cat|kitty|
kitty cat|kitten|feline|pussy cat}} {{is|was|is
always|has been|is usually}}
{{really|truly|quite|extremely|totally}}
{{ugly|hideous|ugly
looking|unsightly|unattractive}}.';
for($i = 1; $i <= 1; $i++)
{
   echo Spinner::detect($string, false).'<br />';
} ?>
```

You can see that we've named out variable $string. Beneath the variable, you'll notice a basic for loop like we discussed earlier.

It basically says that $i equals 1 to start with, and if $i is less than or equal to one, increment $i by 1 and echo out the spun text from our spin function (which we haven't talked about yet).

The Spin Function

We're going to put the code that does the heart of the spinning into another file called spin.php You can see that we've already referenced it on the second line of our PHP code above with the "include" command.

I was going to paste in the code that goes into spin.php, but it ended up being several pages long. So instead of posting it here in the book, I'll just give you a link to it online:

http://johnelder.org/spin.txt

I'm not sure where I came up with that chunk of code, but it spins text nicely.

Just be sure to copy and paste that code into a file called spin.php and upload it to the home directory of your webhosting account (the directory that holds all your web page files).

That's all there is to it!

Be sure to use this sparingly, if at all. Like I said, Google's gotten pretty good at sniffing out spin text and penalizing sites that use it. So if you depend of Google for traffic, you might want to stay away from spinning.

But there are tons of legitimate uses for spin text, and now you have it as a tool in your belt if you need it.

CHAPTER SEVEN

PHP For Wordpress

I build most of my websites with plain old HTML and PHP...and sometimes tack on a Mysql database onto the backend if things get especially complicated.

Setting things up in that way, and using a templating system like I described earlier allows me to scale thousands of websites with relatively small and cheap web hosting accounts.

The reason I don't use Wordpress is because it's a massive resource hog. It takes up a ton of webhosting disk space, and uses a lot more bandwidth than a simple HMTL site ever would.

I have a thousand HTML websites hosted on one simple $50 a month shared VPS account over at **Servint** (**http://www.marketingfool.com/servintrocks.html**).

That same account might be able to successfully host 20-50 wordpress blogs (at the most). So hosting a massive network with thousand of sites is exponentially more expensive if you're going to be using Wordpress.

But most Affiliate Marketers like the ease of use that Wordpress offers, and many people don't necessarily want to run networks of hundreds or thousands of websites.

For them, Wordpress works just fine...but they'd still like to take advantage of some of the tips that I've discussed throughout this book.

Luckily PHP works very well with Wordpress...in fact Wordpress was written in PHP.

Adding PHP To Wordpress Sites

When people try to add PHP to wordpress, they often try to simply add the php code to their posts or pages in the same way they'd add any text, using the wordpress post/page editor.

Unfortunately, that doesn't work. You can type the code into the editor, but it won't execute.

Instead you have to add your code to the actual underlying Wordpress framework php pages.

How Wordpress Works...

Wordpress works similarly to the templating system you just learned in the last chapter.

It splits things up into separate files, and incorporates a database to hold post and page data.

Every time you make a post, Wordpress saves it to the database. When a post page is called on the site, wordpress pulls the post or page data from the database, and slaps it together with the separated template files.

Most Wordpress themes are similarly structured. They usually all have similar basic files. The files you'll want to become familiar with look like this:

header.php
footer.php
index.php
page.php
sidebar.php
single.php
archive.php
404.php
search.php

Not all wordpress themes will name those files that exact way. But they'll name them similarly. Instead of single.php they might name it postsingle.php or themesingle.php or template-single.php But you'll know what it is because it will likely have the word "single" in it.

So what do each of those pages mean? They act mostly the way our templating system from the last chapter acts.

header.php and footer.php will handle the layout for each page or post's header and footer.

index.php will handle the layout of the main webpage of the site.

single.php will handle the layout of a post.

page.php will handle the layout for pages (not posts, but actual page entries).

archive.php will handle the layout for category pages and archives.

404.php will handle error pages (when someone visits a page of your site that doesn't exist).

sidebar.php will handle the code that goes into the sidebar of every post and page of your site.

To use PHP on a wordpress site, you need to add your code to THOSE files directly. You can do that in a couple of different ways.

Method One:

The first method is to FTP (file transfer protocol) into your web host, navigate to the directory that holds those files, and edit them directly using FTP software. I use that method myself because I'm comfortable with FTP software.

Those files are always held in the same place. If your web hosting files are located in the /www/ directory, then those files will be located here:

/www/wp-content/themes/yourtheme/

Each Wordpress theme has a different name and each theme will be located in it's own directory. All the themes that you've uploaded to your Wordpress installation will be located in the /wp-content/themes/ directory.

For instance, if you're using the default twentyeleven theme that comes pre-installed with wordpress, your theme files will be located in this directory:

/www/wp-content/themes/twentyeleven/

Simply navigate to that directory and you'll see a list of all the single.php, header.php, footer.php files etc. Then edit them using your ftp software.

Method Two:

The second, and maybe easier way (especially if you aren't familiar with FTP) is to use Wordpress's "Appearence" editor.

Log into your wordpress installation like you always do to add a post or page or do anything else.

On the left hand menu, click "Appearance" and then "Editor". Depending on what version of Wordpress you're running, it should look a little something like this:

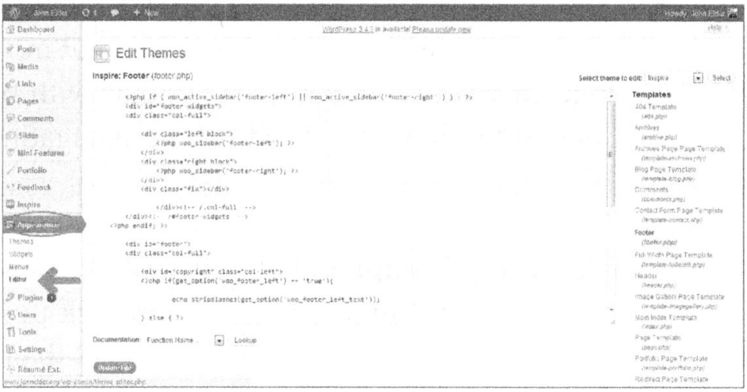

You'll see all the files that make up the theme that you're currently using there on the menu that runs down the right hand side of the screen.

Just click on any of them to edit them. Right now I've got the footer.php pulled up.

All you have to do is add your PHP code into the big gray box in the middle of the screen, then click the "Update File" button below it.

Want to add the PHP year date code we learned earlier? Add it right there to the footer file. You'll have to look through the file and suss out exactly WHERE in that file to put it... and that's where knowing HTML will come into play.

But look at the code that comes up. You'll see that most of it is in PHP that you'll probably be familiar with by now. You shouldn't have too hard a time navigating things.

If you plan on using Wordpress for your web sites, and want to use PHP on it, I highly suggest you pick up a Wordpress book. It'll go into much greater detail than I can in this book.

Even if it's just a "Wordpress for Dummies" book, it's worth the effort. Wordpress has a few quirky things you'll need to learn about, like the Loop (not to be confused with a PHP Loop), that are really beyond the scope of this book.

Method Three

Yeah I said there were two methods, but I suppose there's a third method too.

There are some plugins that you can install that allow you to add your PHP directly to a post or page entry, and there are widgets that allow you to use a sort of shortcode that's meant to mimic php.

I've never used any of those widgets, don't really know anything about them, and don't recommend that you use them.

But I did want to make you aware of them. You can run a search at the Wordpress plugin search page or run a Google search if you're interested in learning more about them.

PHP Limitations On Wordpress

There are some limitations when it comes to PHP and Wordpress. It's hard to make certain PHP code execute on certain specific posts.

When you add PHP code to the single.php file, it will execute on EVERY post that you publish.

You can get around that by adding if/then statements that tie into the wordpress loop. Basically every post you make is given a unique ID, and you can use that ID to run your if/then statement to only execute certain PHP code on certain posts.

But that's a real pain, especially if you want to execute different PHP code on dozens or hundreds of different posts or pages.

You can search the wordpress site to find out exactly how to do it...or better yet, get a Wordpress book and really learn the ins and outs of the system.

Of course, that's going to take some time and effort.

Conclusion

Is it possible to use PHP on wordpress sites, absolutely. But it can be a little tricky depending on how complicated a thing you need to do.

I'll recommend again that you stay away from Wordpress all together. With the skills you've learned from this book, you can build sites with functionality that blows away anything that you can expect from a wordpress site.

And don't forget the savings in webhosting costs over the years. Depending on how large your network is, you could save thousands, or even millions of dollars in web hosting fee's.

CHAPTER EIGHT

Putting It All Together

Well it looks like you made it all the way to the end of the book! Let's take a look at what we've accomplished so far.

You've learned the basics of HTML and FTP, and how PHP ties in with both of them.

You've also learned the basics of PHP; things like:

- delimiters

- the basic structure and syntax of a php statemnt

- how comments are handled and why it's important to use them

And you've also got a pretty solid foundation of basic to intermediate PHP programming concepts; things like:

- Variables

- Comparison Operators

- If / Then Statements

- Loops: For and While

- Randomizing

- Arrays

- Functions

If you master those things, you'll be well on your way to becoming a programmer. Not only will they help you master PHP, but knowing how to handle those things in PHP makes it very easy to learn any different programming languages as well.

We also learned more advanced topics like:

- Templating Websites

- Using PHP on wordpress

I know this was a lot to throw at you in one book. We really covered the gamut from zero to 60mph very quickly, so I hope you'll swing by my personal website at JohnElder.org to drop me an email with any questions you might have.

You can also sign up for my mailing list there (for free) to get notified whenever I'm up to something new.

And be sure to check out my **MarketingFool.com** blog where I talk about Affiliate Marketing in detail, and subscribe to my free daily Adsense newsletter there.

Where To Go From Here?

What's next? Reading a book is one thing, but there's no substitute for getting out there and coding.

I suggest you set up some simple webhosting somewhere (I like Hostgator **http://www.marketingfool.com/hostgatorrocks.html** for cheap hosting) and just start coding!

Start by walking through all of the examples in this book. Try to recreate all the code examples yourself.

Then try to code your own things.

Search around on the Internet and you'll find lots of web sites with coding challenges. They'll give you little problems to try and solve on your own that will sharpen your skills.

I also suggest you scour the Internet for more PHP tutorials and leaning sources. Back in the day you would run out and buy an O'Reilly book on PHP (and I sometimes do that too). But these days you can find most of the information you'll need for free online.

Still, I like to have a good book on hand sometimes that has everything I need at my fingertips. There's something about having a book sitting on your desk, that you can flip through in a snap to find what you need.

Thanks for reading, and good luck!

-John Elder
JohnElder.org

APPENDIX A

Affiliate Marketing Members Only Site

Well you made it all the way to the end of the book, congratulations!

It's a pretty impressive feat!

As a special thank you for purchasing this book and sticking with it to the end, I want to extend an INSANE discount on my special Member's-Only Insiders website where I go into very specific details and teach people how I build a ton of different affiliate websites.

In the last 2 years I've owned over 4,000 Affiliate Marketing websites that have offered millions of products for sale. I've built:

- Thick Adsense Sites

- Thin Adsense Sites

- Portal Websites

- Price Comparison Websites

- Coupon Websites

- Shopping Sites

- Ecommerce Sites

- And more...

And at my members-only site, I show you how to build them all.

But I don't just explain my methods, I give you all the tools and templates to do it yourself.

It's really cool, really hands on, and really helpful to people at all levels of programming or affiliate marketing.

The site is located at:

http://insiders.marketingfool.com

And it's the compliment of my MarketingFool.com website.

Membership isn't cheap, and it shouldn't be. Normally it costs $27 a month ($324 a year) to join and it's worth every penny...

But as a special thank you for buying this book, I'd like to offer you a one-year membership for only $99.

Order Here:
http://www.marketingfool.com/member-special

Membership comes with a TON of stuff.

First and foremost, you get access to my special knowledge library that contains tons of tutorials that walk you through building all kinds of different Affiliate Marketing websites.

But it also contains something special... all the affiliate marketing books I've ever written... available for download...for free.

You'll get:

-Adsense Empire Thick Site Guide
($37 from amazon)

- Adsense Empire Quickstart Guide

($9.99 from amazon)

- Web Page Text Spinning with PHP
($47 from amazon)

- Insiders Affiliate Marketing Guide

And you'll also get every new Affiliate Marketing Book I write in the future, for free.

You also get some pretty cool tools for free too. Things like:

- My Google Quick Index Software that gets new websites indexed in Google within 48 hours.

- My Keyword Tool that helps format lists of keywords into php friendly syntax

- And More...

There's also a members only discussion board where people can ask questions and chat about Affiliate Marketing in a private setting where only serious affiliate marketers hang out.

My Insiders Member's-Only website is a place where I've spilled my guts and deposited all my affiliate marketing knowledge gained through 16 years of successfully making my living online.

If you're serious about making money online, joining this community is a solid step that you won't be sorry to take.

But if you're not satisfied in anyway, just drop me an email and I'll refund 100% of your money with no questions asked.

Take advantage of this special $99 offer, order now:

http://www.marketingfool.com/member-special

Become a Marketing Fool Insider Today! I hope to see you on the inside...

-John Elder
JohnElder.org

APPENDIX B

Resources

Learning to program in any language is largely about learning to become familiar with a set of resources.

No one learns absolutely everything there is to learn about a programming language and keeps it available in their brains at the drop of a hat.

The main reason for that is because many programmers learn multiple languages, even dozens...and those languages change all the time.

They get updated, new features get added, bad features get removed. Part of a programmers job is to constantly be learning new things.

So it's good to become familiar with certain resources for any programming language that you want to learn.

PHP is an open source kind of language so there are lots of free resources on the net for you to take advantage of. I've mentioned some throughout this book, but I thought it would be useful to have a list here at the end of the book that you can look back on in the future.

Resource List:

PHP.net
http://www.php.net
PHP.net is a great resource period. Whenever I look something up at Google, the first couple search results are almost always pointed at php.net.

Not only is it good for explaining different concepts, but people post code examples and discuss things there as well.

The PHP.net Manual:
http://www.php.net/manual/en/langref.php
This is a great manual that allows you to browse through and find what you're looking for. If you know exactly what you're looking for, this is a great place to start.

Google
http://www.Google.com
PHP.net is great, but I usually don't start my search there, I usually start at Google. I might type IF/THEN PHP into Google, and inevitably, the first listing is going to be the php.net page on IF/THEN statements

W3Schools
http://www.w3schools.com/php/
Some people tend to look down on the W3 school as being kind of lame and not a serious programming resource, but I find useful information there all the time, especially for newer programmers. And their website is a little more user friendly than php.net

My Daily Adsense Newsletter
http://www.MarketingFool.com
This is my free daily blog where I talk about different Adsense related Affiliate Marketing topics. I've focused mainly on "thin" adsense sites in the past and there's over 150 articles there to look through, all at no charge.

Insiders Marketing Fool
http://insiders.marketingfool.com
My special member's-only website where I teach people how to build a bunch of different affiliate marketing type websites. It's a great resource with tutorials and site templates, ebooks and hands on help. If you're interested in creating an affiliate marketing network of sites, this is the place for you. (see Appendix A for a deep discount).

Adsense Empire Thick Site Guide
http://www.johnelder.org/adsense.html

My best selling book about building profitable thick authority niche adsense sites. I walk you through an actual case study website and show how I built it from zero to $3,100 in profit with only one week's worth of work. (available for Kindle from Amazon).

My Personal Blog
http://www.JohnElder.org
If you want to keep track of what I'm up to at the moment you can visit my persona blog. There I post articles on web development, starting online businesses, random odds and ends, etc. I've also got a portfolio of most of my past work posted there.

Codecademy Web Fundamentals Class
http://www.codecademy.com/tracks/web
This is a great free learning resource if you're interested in learning HTML and CSS (and even a little javascript). Codecademy is set up like an interactive game that walks you through learning in an easy to follow and fun way. I highly recommend it.

Wordpress
http://www.wordpress.org

For those of you that want to stick with a cms, the wordpress website is a great resource for finding free themes, plugins, and information on tweaking wordpress files and messing with the guts of the program.

A Note From The Author

A SPECIAL REQUEST

If you enjoy this book, would you head back to Amazon.com and leave a quick review or click the "like" button at the top of the page?

(http://www.amazon.com/PHP-Programming-Affiliate-Marketers-ebook/dp/B00A2TTNR0)

Reviews are incredibly important to us independent authors. Just one or two can vault our books up the list at Amazon.com

I'd certainly appreciate it!

-John Elder
JohnElder.org

The End

Made in the USA
Monee, IL
04 November 2026

67387238R00115